MILITARY LAWYERS, CIVILIAN COURTS, AND THE ORGANIZED BAR

MILITARY LAWYERS, CIVILIAN COURTS, AND THE ORGANIZED BAR

A CASE STUDY OF THE UNAUTHORIZED PRACTICE DILEMMA

F. RAYMOND MARKS

AMERICAN BAR FOUNDATION · CHICAGO · 1972

Publication of this work by the
American Bar Foundation signifies that
it is regarded as valuable and responsible.
The analyses, conclusions, and opinions
expressed are those of the author and
not those of the Foundation, its officers
and directors, or others associated with
its work, or of the Army, The Judge
Advocate General, or any other
governmental agency.

Reprinted from 56 *Military Law Review* 1 (1972)

Printed in U.S.A.

The American Bar Foundation

is engaged in research on legal problems and the legal profession. Its mission is to conduct research that will enlarge the understanding and improve the functioning of law and legal institutions. The Foundation's work is supported by the American Bar Association, the American Bar Endowment, The Fellows of the American Bar Foundation, and by outside funds granted for particular research projects.

In 1971 the Department of Defense implemented a pilot program to provide full legal assistance to some of its lower paid members. A key factor in shaping the various state programs was the cooperation or non-cooperation of the local bar associations. The author examines the genesis of the Pilot Legal Assistance Program paying particular attention to military-local bar negotiations. He concludes that in many instances bar resistance was motivated more by economic than by professional concerns.

A recent experimental program of the Department of Defense, seeking to test the feasibility of expanding the nature and scope of legal assistance offered to servicemen and their dependents, has afforded us a unique opportunity to study varying views about delivery of legal services and varying conceptions of the license to practice law and professional responsibility. The experimental program, implemented by each military service through "pilot programs" at a few bases, envisions the delivery of "complete legal services" to certain eligible military personnel and their dependents, including "representation in criminal and civil matters in civilian courts." [1] Moreover, the military legal assistance program seeks to offer this service by having military lawyers appear in civilian

---

[1] On October 26, 1970, Mr. Roger T. Kelley, Assistant Secretary of Defense for Manpower and Reserve Affairs, wrote a Memorandum to the Secretaries of the Military Departments:

The Secretary of Defense desires that you establish a Pilot Program to ascertain the feasibility and desirability of expanding Legal Assistance Programs for military personnel and dependents to provide legal services, *including representation in criminal and civil matters in civilian courts*, to same extent as could be provided by the Office of Economic Opportunity . . .

You are to have the widest possible latitude in conducting the Pilot Programs. Accordingly, only the necessary minimum guidelines have been established by the Office of the Secretary of Defense. . . .

1

courts on behalf of their clients. It is because of this feature that the unauthorized practice of law dilemma is brought into sharp focus; special permission was needed for "foreign lawyers" to practice in local courts.

In actuality, the new pilot programs represent not only an expansion of previously offered legal assistance but involves a contraction in conception as well. What was expanded was the nature and scope of the legal services to be offered. Since 1943 the military has had a legal assistance program (LAP), a program which has given only advice and counseling, has engaged in limited drafting of documents—such as wills, and has offered notarial services.[2] The LAP (old program) does not involve the representation of the servicemen or their dependents; the military lawyer is never counsel of record, nor counsel in the meaningful sense that he can negotiate, plan litigation, litigate, or settle litigation on behalf of a client.[3] The legal assistance officer under the old program refers the client to the civilian bar in instances where full representation is indicated. The new program makes such referrals unnecessary, because the needed representation can be provided directly by the legal assistance officer. In brief, a true lawyer-client relationship is envisioned.

The conceptual contraction involved in the pilot programs is in the definition of those servicemen and dependents who are eligible for the new "fringe benefit" of complete legal service. It is a limited expansion concept. Under the old LAP legal assistance is extended to privates and generals, seamen and admirals alike. The sole test of eligibility has been that the member of the military services be on active duty or in a retired status. The eligibility of dependents follows the eligibility of the servicemen. The guidelines for the new program for the most part restrict eligibility for legal services to enlisted men (and their dependents) who are in pay grade E–4 or below.[4] This restriction is due primarily to an assessment, made at the planning stage, of what was politically possible in terms of eliciting the maximum cooperation from the organized bar and limiting resistance to a minimum. The "compromise" over new pro-

---

[2] For a summary of the historical background and the early operation of the old legal assistance program, *see*: M. BLAKE, LEGAL ASSISTANCE FOR SERVICEMEN (1951).

[3] Recently some of the services have allowed limited negotiation on behalf of clients under the LAP, but it is felt that this step is strongly related to the planning that went into the new pilot programs.

[4] Pay grade E–4 was selected by the military as representing the "poverty line," taking into account pay and the value of benefits. This will be more fully discussed in Part II. The Navy used an E–3 cutoff.

gram eligibility is directly related to the focus of this article: We are concerned here with the way that the military and the organized bar have related to the planned expansion and extension of legal services to a defined group.

This article is about the varying "professional" conceptions of what the license to practice law means to the profession as a whole, the individual license holder, and the public. Because of the ways that the bar and the military have dealt with one another about the pilot programs, issues of who is capable of serving the public or specialized segments of the public, who ought to serve, and how the service should be offered or rendered are raised in clear terms. Unauthorized practice issues are particularly interesting when applied to people trained as lawyers. Data are available about a series of accommodations that remind us of earlier accommodations between the bar and the offerors of legal services to the poor—the legal aid movement and the OEO legal services program. They remind us, too, about the prolonged, recent, and continuing bar resistance to group legal services generally. Moreover, the uniqueness of the proposed military program and the nature of the specific negotiations between the military and several local bar associations enable us to see many of the unauthorized practice of law issues more clearly than in those previous situations.

The attempted expansion of the military legal assistance program—its conversion into a full-scale legal service program—represents the largest closed-panel group legal service in the country.[5] Beyond that, unlike the typical union or poverty group legal service, the professional members of an identifiable group are the designated servers of the nonprofessional members of the same group. In other words, by the new program the military is attempting to "serve its own" with its own. In its essential form the military program is an example of socialized legal services.

The form of implementation of the pilot programs, as has already been mentioned, affords us a good opportunity to isolate issues and

---

[5] It can be argued that the OEO Legal Services Program is the largest group practice in the country. In abstract terms this is true. But in terms of identifying "the clients," for either the serving lawyers or the lawyers who might have served the members of the group in the past, the OEO program lacks the clarity of defined beneficiaries which both the military and union programs have. The beneficiaries of the OEO Legal Services Programs are "the poor." In several instances of specific opposition to the OEO program, local community—neighborhood—lawyers thought they could perceive that the served group embraced "their clients." The general bar, however, did not see their clients involved. In the case of union groups or the military group, the general bar in several communities can identify their clients or potential clients among the beneficiaries of the group plan.

perspectives touching on the meaning of professional role and unauthorized practice. To begin with, the support and cooperation of the American Bar Association was sought—a factor I shall deal with more extensively. When it was received it was in a federated form:

> Resolved, that the American Bar Association *supports the expansion* of existing military legal assistance programs *through the establishment of properly supported pilot, or test program(s) in such states as cooperate and agree with the objectives of giving complete legal services to members of the Armed Forces and their dependents* through the expansion of existing military legal assistance programs, *subject to such limitations*, as to which the Department of Defense and the states and civilian bar associations may agree. . . .[6]

The ABA "approval" underscored the voluntary nature of the national bar—indicating that a statement of norms may be one thing and the power to implement is another. Negotiations between the military services and the bar had to occur with the local bar in those areas where the military desired to establish pilot programs. For our purposes this was fortuitous; we are afforded an opportunity to observe several smaller negotiations and conflicts rather than one symbolic—abstract—conflict. The Department of Defense also indirectly enriched the data base of the study by promulgating broad guidelines for the pilot programs.[7] The guidelines left considerable

---

[6] ABA Board of Governors, Resolution, St. Louis, Missouri, August 13, 1970 (emphasis added).

[7] *See* note 1, *supra*. The Guidelines read:

1. Each military Department is to conduct a Pilot Program. The number and location of individual test programs will be at the discretion of the Secretary concerned.
2. The Military Departments should coordinate their plans to insure that test programs are not concentrated in one geographical area. The widest possible geographical coverage should be insured.
3. Standards of eligibility for recipients of expanded legal services should be coordinated between the Military Departments but such standards do not necessarily have to be identical for test purposes. The basic standard of eligibility is that the recipient of legal services is unable to pay a fee to a civilian lawyer for the services involved without substantial hardship to himself or his family.
4. At least one Military Department should conduct a test program at a location where a tax-supported Public Defender Program and/or a Public, Charitable or Bar supported Legal Aid or Legal Referral Agency is in operation. Working relationships should be established with the Public Defender with respect to the handling of criminal matters in which eligible military personnel and dependents need representation in civilian courts. To the extent feasible, cases involving military personnel and dependents should be referred to the Public Defender for handling.
5. At least one Military Department should conduct a test program at a location where there is the best possible combination of active duty military lawyers, reserve military lawyers, civil service lawyers, and a good climate of cooperation with the civilian bar. For purposes of comparison and evaluation at least one test should be conducted at a location where conditions are less ideal. In establishing such test program, however, it is to be borne in mind that ABA support extends only to the establishment of test programs ". . . in such states as cooperate and

flexibility for each program's ultimate form. Indeed, the forms of the pilot programs, the negotiations with the local bar, and the subsequent revisions of specific programs have been varied. So, too, have the responses of the involved local bars.

It may be that both the military and the local bars have frequently been disingenuous in assigning language and reasons for and against the expanded program, respectively, which obliterate or mask a real source of bar concern—fear of loss of income. Language and negotiations aside, however, the bar's concern about income and the military's awareness of that concern have been a central factor in the shaping and implementation of the new pilot programs for expanded legal assistance. Awareness of probable and actual bar response has permeated the pilot program from the planning stage (at the Pentagon) through the negotiation and implementation stages (at the level of staff judge advocates in the field). For example, in the Department of Defense letter directing implementation we find:

> In all actions taken it should be made clear that the expanded military legal assistance program is not intended to deprive civilian attorneys of sources of income but, to the contrary, is intended to provide legal services for eligible personnel who cannot provide a source of income to the civilian bar.[8]

Notwithstanding the centrality of the income or market issue there are other important concerns which have been voiced and dealt with—on both sides of the bargaining table. Issues were raised about the best way (or the better way) of serving the client group, which in turn touched on the core of the unauthorized practice issue— who is *qualified* to serve the public? And who is not? As we observe these issues, we are afforded an opportunity to apply an analysis of competing professional and counter-professional motives. We are also afforded an opportunity to apply a scale of professionalism ranging from concern over gain to concern over service.[9] We can ask whether those involved see the monopoly granted by the license as a way of protecting the public or a way of advancing the interests of the profession.

---

agree with the objectives of giving complete legal services to members of the Armed Forces and their dependents through the expansion of existing military legal assistance programs. . . ."

[Note: Guideline 3 is quite different—broader—than OEO standards. It may cover most of the military group. I will discuss the implications of this broader guideline in Part II.]

[8] *See* note 1, *supra*, at 2.

[9] The allusion is to Karl Llewellyn's definition: A profession puts service ahead of gain. *See*: Llewellyn, *The Bar Specializes—With What Results?* 167 ANNALS 177 (1933). It may be an illusion as well as an allusion.

Another feature of this study assures us that an examination of military-bar negotiations will produce significant insights into the views of the legal profession—particularly the organized bar—about the license to practice. That is the following cluster of facts: licenses are required to practice law in most jurisdictions; [10] military lawyers are not usually licensed to practice law in the jurisdictions where they are based; in some jurisdictions the organized bar has autocratic power to determine who may practice in the courts, and, in other jurisdictions, the bar has substantial influence—principally with the courts—toward the same end.[11] In a significant way, then, this article is about the ways that the power to license—or influence licensing—is used and abused.

We examine first the deliberations of the military that led to the selection of the particular approach to expanded legal services for servicemen. This includes a view of the alternatives facing the military planners as well as a view both of the predictions made about the needs, positions, and possible objections of the organized bar and what initial steps were taken by the military to alleviate or ameliorate the "opposition"—i.e., to secure bar cooperation. We then examine the specific military-bar negotiations leading to or frustrating the implementation of pilot programs at particular bases and in particular jurisdictions. Finally, we view the process and the issues from an overall perspective.

I. THE PLANS OF THE MILITARY

While the Department of Defense, since 1967, had been considering the expansion of the military legal assistance program, no direct action toward that end was taken until after Congress, in December 1969, passed the Carey Amendment to the Economic Opportunity Act of 1964.[12] (The Carey Amendment provided for the extension

---

[10] This is not universal. The Coast Guard, in seeking to implement its pilot program in the First Coast Guard District, found that no order of court would be required for cases where service lawyers represent servicemen in New Hampshire courts. Sec. 311:1 of the NEW HAMPSHIRE REVISED STATUTES (1966) provides: "A party in any cause or proceeding may appear, plead, prosecute, or defend, in his proper person *or by any citizen of good character.*" (Emphasis supplied.)

[11] The medical program of the armed services, offering full range medical services to *all* members of the armed forces and their dependents, never has had to run the licensing gauntlet now faced by the legal service program. Most medical services are performed at federal facilities, beyond the jurisdiction of licensing authorities.

[12] S. 3016, 91st Cong., 1st Sess. (1969) (Carey Amendment), amended para. 222(a)(3) of the Economic Opportunity Act by adding:
Members of the Armed Forces, and members of their immediate families, shall be eligible to obtain legal services under such programs [OEO Programs] in cases

6

of legal services by the OEO to military "hardship" personnel and their dependents.) The military's earlier consideration had been prompted principally by concern over the inability to attract and retain lawyers. A Working Group on Military Lawyer Procurement, Utilization, and Retention saw an expanded legal assistance program as a way of offering attractive and competing professional career options to the military lawyer. That Group recommended that the Department of Defense:

> Study the feasibility and desirability of [seeking cooperation from the American Bar Association and State Bar Associations with a view toward] defining areas in which Legal Assistance Officers would be permitted to prepare and file pleadings in civilian courts, negotiate . . . in behalf of clients, and, in certain cases, make court appearances in behalf of clients.[13]

Congressional action, which was neither sought nor welcomed by the military,[14] forced at least a partial shift of emphasis in the approach to expanded service from consideration of the lawyers to a consideration of alternative ways of serving the clients. This did not mean, however, that subsequent discussion necessarily became client-centered. The military had its needs, too, and legal services continued to be discussed, in terms of these needs, as a tactical deployment of a fringe benefit—as an implementation of an overall strategy for the retention of personnel.[15] Delivery of legal service was discussed in a context of an all-volunteer force.

---

of extreme hardship (determined in accordance with regulations of the Director issued after consultation with the Secretary of Defense) : *Provided*, That nothing in this sentence shall be so construed as to require the Director to expand or enlarge existing programs or to initiate new programs in order to carry out the provisions of this sentence unless and until the Secretary of Defense assumes the cost of such services and has reached agreement with the Director on reimbursement for all such additional costs as may be incurred in carrying out the provisions of this sentence.

[13] Report of Department of Defense Military Working Group on Expansion of Legal Assistance Programs [hereinafter referred to as "McCartin Report" after the group chairman, Colonel George J. McCartin, Jr.], Sec. IA1, which cites the earlier Working Group on Military Lawyer Procurement, Utilization and Retention; and McCartin Report, Enclosure 1.

[14] The military was not the only affected party left in the blind; the OEO did not seek and did not know of the Amendment until it was before the House-Senate Conference Committee. The history of the Carey Amendment is obscure.

[15] The shift in focus may have been somewhat illusory. The two concerns—desire to attract and hold the military lawyer and desire to find the best ways of serving the client group—are very much related to a single overall concern about the manpower base. There was a shift from reliance on the draft or, as in the case of the Navy, draft-induced enlistments, to considerations of a volunteer force. Earlier the Gates Commission had suggested that the keys to a volunteer military force were: attractive career options, competitive wages, including *fringe benefits*, and morale. Of course, the first two elements have an important bearing on the third—morale.

Congressional action had another effect, this one having profound and far-reaching consequences. By addressing only those servicemen and their dependents who were eligible for assistance from OEO Legal Services Programs—"the hardship cases"[16]—the Carey Amendment forced a fractionalized consideration of the client group; it had the effect of reinforcing an historical basis for a compromise with the civilian bar.[17] Group legal services might be tolerable to the bar to the extent that the extended service would not interfere with service that the bar was already rendering to an established clientele—its paying clients.

The Carey Amendment contained two harsh realities for the planners in the Pentagon: (1) there was the threat of a legislative finding that some members of the armed services were living below the "poverty line," and (2) there was also a threat of finding that the military was neither the exclusive nor necessarily the best resource for supplying its members with needed or desirable goods and services. Both findings had implications that the military could not or should not "take care of its own." The fact that both issues strongly related to adequacy of military pay scales and acceptance by Congress of the professional status of military careers was of small comfort. It was difficult to talk of careers and poverty at the same time.

Reactions to the Carey Amendment ranged from feelings of stigma[18] to feelings of intrusion. The official reaction was quick and singular. During the pendency of the amendment, letters were sent to key Congressmen by the Secretary of Defense[19] and by the Acting General Counsel of the Department of Defense[20] expressing opposition to the amendment on the grounds that the existing legal assistance program was the natural vehicle for meeting the need perceived by the amendment, even if that entailed an expanded or altered form of the assistance program. The letter written by the Acting General Counsel (at the request of Secretary Laird) is of particular note. Counsel said, in part:

---

[16] 115 CONG. REC. 40401 (1969) (remarks of Senator Peter Dominick).

[17] By "force" I do not mean that the Carey Amendment foreclosed consideration of the entire military group.

[18] One military lawyer stated, in an interview with the author: "Although our lower grade enlisted people were eligible for charity services, we considered that it was demeaning to send a man in uniform to have him wait hours in the outside office of some charitable legal service and mingle with the desperately poor people."

[19] Letter from Melvin Laird to L. Mendel Rivers, Chairman, House Committee on Armed Services, Dec. 20, 1969.

[20] Letter from L. Niederlehner to Representative Albert H. Quie, Nov. 19, 1969.

8

Admittedly [the existing programs] have certain limitations which impair their effectiveness and make it impossible for complete legal services to be provided. One of the more significant limitations is that the military legal officers in the main are limited to providing office advice, including preparation of some legal documents, and are unable to represent their clients in court proceedings or other legal proceedings or to negotiate fully in their behalf with adversaries. These *limitations* are due to a number of factors *including the attitude of the organized civilian bar regarding such matters.* These restrictions have been a source of concern and some frustration to military legal officers who would like to provide more complete legal services to their clients.[21]

Citing the military lawyer procurement study, the letter went on:

One of the recommendations of the study group proposed that efforts be made, in cooperation with civilian bar associations, to expand the military legal assistance programs so that military legal officers could provide more complete legal services to military personnel—*in particular those in the lower enlisted pay grades.*[22]

The cited procurement study did not single out the lower pay grades! That suggestion appears for the *first* time in the letter of the Acting General Counsel. This letter thus represented the first adoption by the military of a fractionalized view of the client group. Was this a concession to the focus of the amendment or to the attitude of the civilian bar cited by Counsel? Or was there yet a third reason—the serious shortages of dollar and manpower reserves that would be needed if the old assistance program were converted to a full service program for *all?* The excuse given by Congress may have been welcomed. The thought of actually extending expanded service to all may have produced a willingness to fracture the group.

Shortly after the passage of the Carey Amendment, the Department of Defense notified the Director of the Bureau of the Budget that it would take *no* steps to implement the law—i.e., that it would not, under the proviso, make arrangements with the OEO to reimburse that agency for legal services extended to military personnel—but that it would "continue to consider the problems to which [the Amendment] is addressed."[23]

The Working Group on Expansion of Legal Assistance, under the chairmanship of Colonel George J. McCartin, Jr. (Army Representative), was formed by directive from the Office of the Assistant Secretary of Defense on March 4, 1970.[24] There were also representa-

---

[21] *Id.* (emphasis added).

[22] *Id.* at 2 (emphasis added).

[23] Letter from L. Niederlehner to Robert Mayo, Dec. 24, 1969.

[24] Memorandum from Roger T. Kelley to Assistant Secretaries of the Military Departments (Manpower and Reserve Affairs), Mar. 4, 1970.

tives from the Navy, the Air Force, and the Coast Guard.[25] The
DOD charge to the group was not as broad as the title of the group
suggests:

> [S]tudy in depth the possible expansion of military legal assistance
> programs in keeping with [prior study group recommendations], *and
> in furtherance of the Department of Defense position taken in connec-
> tion with the recent [Carey] amendment. . . .*[26]

This seems to be a directive that the amendment be forsworn and
that the earlier directive—to consider the use of military lawyers in
civilian courts—be pursued. The "Objectives and Suggested Areas of
Study" accompanying the March 4, 1970 directive make it clear that
the gloss of intervening political exchange was added to any further
consideration of expanded legal services. The objectives included:

> [T]o determine the extent to which such expansion of service is
> feasible; *to define* the types and scope of such expanded services and
> *persons who would be eligible* . . .[27]

The terms "eligible" and "eligibility" seemed embedded in the
dialogue right from the start; the threat of outside legal service to
military personnel on an organized basis and the "natural" limitations seen to derive from the attitudes of the civilian bar would limit
the study group's efforts to a search for *tolerable alternatives*.

The areas of study and examination "suggested" by the Assistant
Secretary of Defense included: (1) an estimate of the number of
people who would be served; (2) "the kind of legal service military
personnel and dependents are eligible for through the Office of Economic Opportunity"; (3) the type of cases then handled by legal
assistance officers and a review of the number and type of cases then
being referred to the civilian bar by legal officers under the old legal
assistance program and the pay grades of the military clients so
referred; (4) the number of military lawyers required in "an expanded" program; (5) estimated effect of expanded legal services
from the viewpoint of overall morale and retention rates; (6) "Desirability and feasibility of providing such expanded legal assistance
with military attorneys compared to funding OEO, together with
comparative costs"; (7) utilization of interservice exchange on a
geographical basis to handle representation in civil courts;[28] (8)

---

[25] The Coast Guard here is treated as a military department, even though its
dominant mission is law enforcement and its organizational setting puts it in
the Department of Transportation and not in the Department of Defense. *See
also* 14 U.S.C. § 1 (1970).

[26] *See* note 24 *supra* (emphasis added).

[27] *Id.*, "Objectives and Suggested Areas of Study," sec. 1.

[28] Note that the term "civil court," as used by the military, means nonmilitary
court and includes civil and criminal jurisdiction.

10

"Possibility of utilizing military and civilian attorneys under a joint participation or sponsorship program"; (9) *"The necessity and means of obtaining cooperation from the American Bar Association and State and local bars"*; (10) the impact which adoption of the Gates Commission recommendations for an all volunteer Armed Force would have on an expanded legal assistance program; and (11) "the views of Staff Judge Advocates, legal officers and legal assistance officers." [29]

The McCartin Report was submitted to the Assistant Secretary of Defense within four months of the original request, just in time for Colonel McCartin to seek the cooperation of the American Bar Association at its annual meeting in St. Louis in August 1970. It was an impressive review of the issues on often meager data. The records on the old legal assistance program, for example, were, when extant, incomplete or unreliable.[30] Other issues admittedly called for subjective judgments. The McCartin Report is in the form of answers to the questions implied by the "Objectives and Suggested Areas of Study." The findings and recommendations turned on three crucial issues: (a) availability of dollar and manpower resources for an expanded program; (b) a set of judgments as to whether the military lawyer or the civilian lawyer was in the best position to extend complete services to military personnel—this included an assessment of whether the civilian lawyer had in the past rendered such service or would in the future, and it included a view that service included understanding and empathy; and (c) assessments about the importance of obtaining civilian bar approval and the extent to which bar cooperation was possible—i.e., how far would civilian bar tolerance toward an expanded legal service program go?

The critical findings were: [31]

    (a) The present program [old legal assistance program] was available to somewhere between 9.5 and 10 million people.[32]

    (b) The old program had changed little since its inception in 1943, *except that there was no regular cooperation from the civilian bar or voluntary participation by the civilian bar as there had been at the beginning.* The program was too limited to provide desirable levels of service. . . .

---

[29] *See* note 24, *supra*, sec. 4 (emphasis added). The list either paraphrases or quotes of some of the items.

[30] Based on the author's personal observations.

[31] The findings are lettered according to the McCartin Report and are either paraphrased or quoted, as indicated with emphasis added.

[32] The notion of eligibility was present in the old program only on the fringes. All active duty personnel could receive the services by definition. There remained the problem of defining the secondary groups: "dependents," "retired" status (eligible), nonactive reservists (not eligible).

(d) There are 2,334,305 persons included in, and dependent on, active duty service in pay grade E–4 and below.

(e) There is no specific statutory basis for the present military Legal Assistance Programs beyond the needs of "welfare" and "efficiency"!
. . .

(q) The supply of the new lawyer requirements alone will not suffice to accomplish any appreciable expansion of the program. . . .

(r) (1) The estimated effects of expanded legal services on "overall" morale would be good, if "conservatively and carefully publicized as 'the services taking care of their own' *avoiding the impression that the military lawyers are taking business (and money) from the civilian bar.*"

(2) The estimated effects on retention rates as a "fringe benefit" would be good.

(3) Specifically, the ability to hold onto trained men who might, because of debts and personal worries and inability to receive legal assistance for their relief, leave the service or seek administrative discharge, would be enhanced.

(s) (1) It is "more desirable to provide expanded legal assistance with military lawyers or a combination of military lawyers and service employed civilian lawyers than funding O.E.O. services." This finding is based on accessibility of lawyers—the military version of the outreach program, a base being the serviceman's neighborhood—and the effect such convenience would have on the lawyer-client relationship, on client and troop morale, and on costs to the military for time and travel away from the post.

(2) The feasibility of providing an expanded program of court appearances depends on the ability of the Department of Defense to support the program and "*the extent to which states, courts, and bar will permit its expansion.*"

(t) There is not only a possibility but a necessity of interservice exchange of lawyers, both active duty and reservists, on a geographical basis.

(u) "The use of a combination of additional military and civilian lawyers who are non-active duty reservists would enhance the expansion of the program and" avoid some of the problems connected with the courts and bar objections and would lend assistance in obtaining necessary permissions.

(v) The program would render all types of services "to the extent the states, courts, and bar cooperate."

(y) "*The state courts and bar associations, together with the American Bar Association, must be persuaded of the need for, and the quality and extent of the program . . .* and of *the absence of any intent to take legitimate business from the civilian bar, indicating recognition of the need for the availability and expansion of legal services even beyond the poverty level recognized by the American Bar Association, its president and many writers.*"

The "findings" of the McCartin group were indeed a mixed bag. They covered items of hard data, such as relative costs of delivering different types of legal service, numbers of people served by the legal assistance program in the past and expected to be served in the future, and estimates of the numbers of people eligible for past and future services. The findings also embraced a wide range of matters which rested on opinion, such as philosophies about a volunteer army and personal services as fringe benefits; views about the impact of an expanded program on troop and lawyer morale; and judgments about the superiority or desirability of having military lawyers serve the civil legal needs of military personnel rather than having civilian lawyers serve those needs and the degree of cooperation that could be expected from both the organized bar and individual lawyers. The opinions in these areas often rested on personal preferences and professional outlook—i.e., the professional soldier's or sailor's outlook or the military lawyer's outlook. The element permeating these findings, however, is the view that bar cooperation was necessary and that it stopped at the water's edge of the economics of law practice. This permeating effect is most dramatically illustrated in finding (r)(i). There the finding concerns itself with the effect of the expanded program on troop morale and the importance of an adjunctive program of "conservative publicity." Then, as if an afterthought—but not really—the cautionary note is added, "avoiding the impression that military lawyers are taking business (and money) from the civilian bar." The central subject of the finding becomes strained, just as the overall findings themselves became strained, between the pulls of rendering a service—distributing a fringe benefit—and the "political" limitations deriving from the Working Group's views about the attitudes of the organized bar toward licensing and toward institutionalized offering of legal services. In finding (r)(i) the Group was saying that morale can be benefited by an expanded legal service program, *provided* the process does not awaken the sleeping giant—the organized bar.

On a broader level, the dissonance observed in finding (r)(i) was repeated many times—frequently more subtly—when questions of availability of legal counsel and access to the legal process had to be considered also in terms of the possibly conflicting interest—self-interest—of the bar as a whole. On the issue of eligibility alone, the predetermined nature of the findings is apparent. As Colonel Mc-Cartin, chairman of the Working Group, has stated:

> If we gave it to everybody that would mean a sizable dent in the local bar's pocket. We knew we would never be able to get away with it. We knew we had to get the cooperation of the local bar. So, since it was OEO and its entering the picture that forced us into this position, we figured we would be able to furnish the service or comply with the Congressional mandate.[33]

---

[33] Interview with Colonel George McCartin. May 4, 1971.

In a way, the conflict, seen as affecting the considerations of the McCartin Committee and perhaps compelling its ultimate recommendation that expanded service be offered only to those under the poverty line, had been present for some time prior to any formal considration of expanded legal services. It simply had not been faced explicitly. The conflict can be seen as more basic, as a clash between two professional outlooks—those of the military profession and of the legal profession. Further, there was an element of identical interest which seemed to move conflict from the subtle to the aggravated form. Both professions would start to talk about legal services as either necessitous or desirable, and, as that necessity was assumed or was treated as apparent, issues of *who* should render service and *how* that service should be rendered would emerge as threats to each.

As early as 1943 a War Department Circular stated:

> Legal assistance offices will be established as soon as possible and wherever practicable, throughout the Army, *so that military personnel can obtain gratuitous legal service* from volunteer civilian lawyers and from lawyers who are in the military service. *Such gratuitous legal service should not be considered as charity but entirely as a service of the same nature as medical, welfare, or other similar services provided for military personnel. In any proper case the legal assistance office may refer the serviceman to civilian counsel for retention by the serviceman upon the usual civilian basis.*[34]

The directive is instructive. An attempt was made to analogize legal services to medical services, already socialized for members of the military profession, while at the same time recognizing that such status was aspirant rather than secure. There was also a recognition of the distinction between the military way of delivering these services and the "usual civilian basis" but as yet no recognition of a conflict regarding legal services. That would have to await events such as community discussion about the necessity of legal services which accompanied, for the poor at least, the advent of OEO Legal Services.

In sum, and to recapitulate, the recommendations of the McCartin group—which followed the "findings"—that military lawyers should be licensed to provide full-range legal service to military personnel under grades E–4, and their dependents, and that bar cooperation was both desirable and necessary seems to have been a foregone conclusion even before the Group met, even before they considered alternative ways of expanding services, and even before the Carey Amendment provided the excuse for fractionalizing that service.

---

[34] *See* M. BLAKE, note 2 *supra*, at 62 (emphasis added).

The low level advice and counseling program which the military had operated since 1943 had not generated any substantial opposition, although both the unauthorized practice of law elements and the inexorable conflict between philosophies of delivering services to a group were present from the beginning. The fact that the supply of legal services had, in the past, been viewed by the offerors of the service as nonnecessitous—as extras—as distinct from the supply of services like medicine, helped to avoid the recognition of the conflict. So, too, did the relative invisibility and marginality of the services as viewed by outsiders [35]—particularly the legal profession as a whole and those within the profession. But, as the community and the profession began to debate supplying legal services as a necessity or a near necessity, the conflict became explicit—it involved competing views of institutionalized delivery of services. It was at this juncture that the military profession's view that goods and services ought to be distributed on a socialized basis could be seen clearly and as a possible threat to the legal profession. It this context, the central question raised by the McCartin report is made clearer:

> The challenge now is: Will states and bar associations allow the military lawyer to do more for his military clients when they need it, and if so, how much? [36]

The split of the eligible group has already been seen as a concession to political reality, with some economic basis as well. Nevertheless, when it was recommended it drew a sharp dissent from Lieutenant Commander Charles Martin, the Coast Guard representative. His dissent further describes the conflict of professional outlooks that we have been discussing:

> [The recommendation that expanded legal services be limited to pay grades E-4 and below is subject to some objections.] *The traditional concept of a military organization as a "band of brothers"* and 27 years of equal treatment in legal assistance for all officers and men and their dependents strongly contraindicates the adoption of the civilian concept of "Poverty" levels within the armed forces as a criteria for determining eligibility for *any* benefits which benefits thus become inescapably categorized as "Charity." The mere recognition of "poverty levels" in the military runs counter to that touchstone of *military professionalism*, the maxim: "The service looks after its own." . . . Suc-

---

[35] The term "outsiders" will be helpful. We shall see it later: members of the military profession will be viewed as outsiders by the bar in a particular locale and vice versa, with the military lawyer being viewed as an outsider to both—or an insider, depending on the circumstances.

[36] McCartin Report, sec. II, B, 3.

cess and motivation for the first time would result in being denied a
fringe benefit. . . .

The only appropriate standard for the administration of such benefits is to ask "Is he one of ours?" and if so we have a duty to look
after him and his.[37]

Commander Martin's remarks put the issue out front: "[It]
would be best not to provide any expansion of legal service at all
rather than limiting such expansion. . . ."[38] In other words, how far
would the military change its conception of the distribution of
goods and services to accommodate the felt political realities of the
organized bar?

The awkwardness of the squeeze between traditional military notions of how goods and services ought to be distributed and the
political realities of bar "permission" or veto is illustrated by the dissonance between two "findings" in the McCartin report. On the one
hand the Group found:

Politically and practically it would be unwise for the Department to
attempt any expansion which the bench and bar do not approve and
then permit.[39]

At the very same time, however, speaking of the old program—
LAP—the Group said:

The continuation of our present program is a must, otherwise morale
will suffer and the expansion would become a cause of dissension and
discord. *To offer an expanded program to a few at the expense of the
many career-oriented personnel who receive the present limited legal
assistance would be most unwise and do harm rather than good.*[40]

A paradox is apparent. The subfinding regarding the old program
is precisely the point that Commander Martin made in his comments
about the new program. Where, then, in its planning for the expansion of a program which had existed since 1943, and about which
there seems to have been a cohesive view, did the Working Group pick
up a vulnerability to bar veto which caused an abandonment of this
cohesive approach? Was it avoidable?

To answer the latter question first—Was vulnerability to bar veto
and overdependence on bar cooperation avoidable?—one should first
look at the history of the old legal assistance program. Regardless of
what was said or regardless of the felt need to "cooperate with the

---

[37] *Id.*, Expanded Coast Guard Comments. appended to sec. III, Findings and
Recommendations (emphasis added).

[38] *Id.*

[39] McCartin Report, sec II, C, 6, a.

[40] *Id.* (emphasis added).

16

private bar"—arising perhaps out of the military lawyer's membership in two brotherhoods (the military profession and the legal profession)—the old program was not vulnerable. That does not mean, however, that there was not some exposure to unauthorized practice of law rules or charges that unauthorized practice was involved. The exposure was there.

The legal assistance officer who "advised" a general or private about a house purchase and examined papers pertaining to the purchase, or gave estate planning advice, including, in many instances, the drafting of a will, was frequently seen as practicing law without the necessary licenses in many jurisdictions.[41] Three factors of immunity, however, made this exposure minimal—merely technical. First, the "law offices" where the advice and counseling and sometimes drafting services were rendered were, for the most part, outside of the jurisdiction of most states—on federal military reservations. The United States Congress—and courts—have exclusive jurisdiction over such territory [42] unless there was a reservation of jurisdiction by agreement with a state at the time of cession or condemnation or unless Congress shall have subsequently relinquished exclusive jurisdiction.[43] There is no evidence that the states had ever reserved, or the Congress had ever relinquished, jurisdiction over the practice of law on military reservations. Nor is there evidence of any attempt by a state bar or a state court to attempt to exercise jurisdiction over the practice of law on military reservations—and other federal installations.[44] The practice of law on military reservations has been, therefore, like the practice of medicine at such installations, free from state regulation and from meaningful regulation by the organized bar.[45]

---

[41] This same charge has been leveled at house counsel to large national corporations.

[42] Article I, Section 8, Clause 17 of the United States Constitution provides that Congress shall have the power:

To exercise exclusive Legislation in all Cases . . . over all Places purchased by the Consent of the Legislature of the State in which the Same shall be, for the Erection of Forts, Magazines, Arsenals, Dock-Yards, and other Needful Buildings ; . . .

See Paul v. United States, 371 U.S. 245 (1963). In subsequent discussion we shall see that the Leavenworth County bar in Kansas used the extraterritorial argument as a basis for attempting to block a Kansas lawyer in the Army JAG Corps from practicing in local Kansas courts.

[43] See James Stewart & Co., Inc. v. Sadrakula, 309 U.S. 94 (1940).

[44] This is not to say that Federal Courts do not review legal proceedings on federal property.

[45] At times when state medical licensing boards evidenced hostility to "foreign doctors," this exemption from state regulation enabled the Veterans Administration to staff its hospitals with foreign, unlicensed doctors.

Second, the law work done at military reservations, as long as it did not involve court appearances by the military lawyer, was either invisible to the civilian bar or, where visible, it was viewed as adjunctive to the work of the civilian bar. By invariably referring court work, matters calling for direct representation, and matters needing services beyond the scope of the legal assistance officer's advice and counseling, the legal assistance officer insured a view, by the private bar, that the old program was simply engaged in screening and workups of paying business. The civilian bar could view the military lawyer as brokers of business. In this context, the chance of anger or dismay over the drafting of wills or other intrusions into the domain of the private lawyer was both permissible and pardonable, particularly since it was in lieu of referral or solicitor's fees. The LAP was viewed as creating complementary dollar demand for legal services, not as competitive. To be sure, frequently the civilian bar was offered cases that did not generate fees. What happened when this occurred—when burdens and not benefits were distributed—was an important but separate issue. The argument has been made that default on the part of the civilian bar to handle nonfee or reduced-fee cases was one of the factors that forced an expanded legal service program on the military.

The third reason why the old LAP was not vulnerable to bar veto is related to the first reason: Simply, bar permission was not needed to conduct the advice and counseling program. There was no affirmative action that was either necessary or desirable.

It is doubtful whether an expanded legal service program—involving full-scale representation of clients—per se involves greater vulnerability to bar veto or limitation. Vulnerability seems to turn on whether the three special factors of immunity—jurisdiction, invisibility, and bar permission not needed—are altered or abandoned. If an expanded program did not contemplate the use of military lawyers, or the escalation of the role of military lawyer from screener and referrer and, perhaps, counselor to that of advocate, representative, and more particularly counsel of record, there seems to be no basis for assuming that the organized bar would or could effectively object to or limit such program. Exposure then seems to turn on how an expanded legal service program affects the military lawyer's role. The Working Group considered several options which would not have affected the role of the military lawyer. These included:

A. Judicare—a plan whereby a serviceman or his dependents could go to a civilian lawyer of his choice and the plan would pay scheduled fees to that lawyer.

B. Direct contract with certain members of the civilian bar for the benefit of the eligible personnel. In this instance the military would choose the lawyer.

C. Acceptance of the Carey Amendment, letting OEO Legal Service Programs represent eligible military personnel, and making payments to the OEO for the service rendered.

D. Employment of civilian lawyers, licensed in the jurisdiction of their service, as house legal assistance lawyers.

E. The use of locally admitted military reservists on a non-fee basis, where the reservist would earn active duty pay and retirement credit.

F. Continuation or expansion of the existing referral patterns, but without military intervention regarding fees.

It is doubtful whether the adoption of any of the options for *all* military and their dependents would have either aroused the civilian bar or would have required the degree of cooperation and agreement from the bar and bench that the plan adopted finally required. Not only would the role of the active-duty military lawyer remain exempt under each of the options—he would still be performing screening and referral services—but in each option a civilian attorney, already admitted to practice in the jurisdiction, would be counsel of record. To be sure, as the group was seen to include potential fee-generating matters, options B, D, and E would have greater political difficulty with the organized bar, because of their closed-panel or group legal service elements. But the greater "difficulty" would not amount to vulnerability because of three United States Supreme Court decisions [46] and the revision of the legal profession's code of professional responsibility.[47] The Code of Professional Responsibility, recommended by the American Bar Association in July 1969 and adopted as of December 31, 1971 in 41 states and approved in 7 more is directly in point. It provides, in Disciplinary Rule 2–103(D):

> A lawyer shall not knowingly assist a person or organization that recommends, furnishes, or pays for legal services to promote the use of his services or those of his partners or associates. *However, he may cooperate in a dignified manner with the legal service activities of any of the following, provided that his independent professional judgment is exercised in behalf of his client without interference or control by any organization or person: . . .*

---

[46] NAACP v. Button, 371 U.S. 415 (1963), Brotherhood of Railroad Trainmen v. Virginia *ex rel.* Virginia State Bar, 377 U.S. 1 (1964) ; and United Mine Workers of America, District 12 v. Illinois State Bar Association, 389 U.S. 217 (1967). Since the McCartin Group met, there has been a fourth case which upholds the group offering of legal services. United Transportation Union v. State Bar of Michigan, 401 U.S. 576 (1971).

[47] Code of Professional Responsibility, DR 2–103 (d) (2).

(2) A military legal assistance office.[48]

The current professional or corporate view of the organized bar, in other words, contemplates and sanctions the cooperation of members of the civilian bar with military legal assistance programs. It exempts the military program from the general strictures regarding group service. To be sure, the drafters of the Code of Professional Responsibility did not contemplate the pilot program. Only the old LAP was contemplated. The language of the Code, however, is broad.

Option F, the continuation of the existing program, without government payment on account of the members of the group, is of course, nothing but a referral service, even if the scope of advice and counseling short of "representation" were expanded.[49] Option F, however, fell considerably short of the view that a fringe benefit ought to be distributed. It was nothing more than "we will help you find a lawyer who you can pay if you can afford it." Accordingly, the McCartin Group was able to dismiss this option easily; something more had to be given. Note, however, that the chosen expansion had the effect of leaving option F in effect for those in pay grades higher than E–4. For potential fee payers, the military legal assistance program would continue to operate as a screening and referral program.

Options A (judicare), B (contract payments), and D (use of government employed civilian lawyers as house counsel—staff legal service lawyers) were rejected by the McCartin Group principally on a cost basis. The Group found, not surprisingly, that military lawyers cost less than civilian lawyers.[50] There were, however, two additional reasons for the rejection: (1) the military lawyer would not benefit from an expanded role—as an intake and referring lawyer there would be no professional challenge, and (2) an effective counseling program, even short of court appearances, required an ability to directly negotiate for the client, an ability to close matters at the earliest and cheapest point. We must recall, when considering why the group rejected options which would not change the role of military lawyers, that both the Defense Department charge to the McCartin Group and the past consideration of expanded legal service posed the problem of lawyer morale and lawyer retention as well as troop morale and retention. It is not surprising that the McCartin Group altered the role of the military lawyers.

---

[48] *Id.* (emphasis added).

[49] Lawyers may, of course, cooperate with bar operated or bar approved lawyer referral services. *See* Code, DR 2–103(D)(4).

[50] McCartin Report, Section II, 6 (f).

20

The second point here has a bearing on both issues—there are real and psychological benefits to both troops and lawyers in being able to "solve problems" rapidly. The point regarding role is summarized in a letter to the Working Group from the Director of the Ohio State Legal Services Association:

> I agree with Colonel McCartin when he says that the legal assistance officers are in poor bargaining position due to the fact that they are not permitted to file any pleadings or make any court appearances.[51]

The ability to bargain and settle is enhanced by the ability to follow through. So, too, both the lawyer's and client's view of the military lawyer's role are enhanced by this ability to follow through. This has morale consequences.

Beyond these specific reasons for recommending against plans involving the use of the civilian bar, the McCartin Group also felt a disenchantment with the unevenness of service rendered by the civilian bar under the old legal assistance program. The Group felt that greater quality control and more stable service—free from the viscissitudes of acceptance or rejection of cases on an *ad hoc* basis—could be achieved by use of military lawyers. As we shall see later in more detail, this parochialism and confidence of the Judge Advocates in their own certification and selection process comes into sharp conflict with the parochialism of several local bars and their confidence in *their* certification process—i.e., licensing.

Concern about the evenness of service offered by OEO was also a factor in the McCartin Group's rejection of option C. The Group surveyed OEO eligibility standards around the country and found vast differences in income eligibility criteria. They also found that the OEO offices varied greatly from place to place in the scope of service rendered—the nature of cases and matters taken. From the military planner's viewpoint, this state of events left them with a problem as to how to draw nationwide guidelines for use of OEO legal services,[52] a problem seen to have morale consequences. Not only, then, would hardship distinguish eligibility for a fringe benefit within the military group, but there would be an additional dissonance around the question, "Who is a hardship case?" The military could not easily draw a differential standard. The Group suggested that an approach to the Director of OEO Legal Services for a directive to local projects could perhaps reduce the application of local differential rules to servicemen and their dependents.[53] How-

---

[51] *Id.*, enclosure 23.
[52] *Id.*, sec. II, C, 2.
[53] *Id.*, sec. II, C, 2, i.

ever, this suggestion did not meet other concerns about OEO serving military personnel. While not explicit, the McCartin Group showed strong feelings about the OEO dispensing a largesse to servicemen, even if paid for under the Carey Amendment. Moreover, the Group had a serious question about whether servicemen and their dependents—not really members of the local community—would be treated, even by OEO, as second-class recipients of that service. Here, of course, it should be noted that some of the same feelings were expressed about the treatment received or expected by "outsider" military personnel at the hands of local private lawyers. There were feelings of strains or possible strains in military-community relations. These feelings were not new, but the military indicated a particular vulnerability.[54] Rejection of the OEO option rested, in part, with the sense that the OEO could not possibly understand the needs of the military personnel as well as the military itself[55] and might be indifferent at best or hostile at worst. In part, this same sensitivity expressed about civilian lawyers explains the rejection of the other options involving the use of civilian lawyers:

> In a "popular war" or one involving the entire country and its resources, the cooperation and attitude of the civilian lawyer is a far different thing from that evidenced during time of peace or during an unpopular war.[56]

The military planners also felt that the military lawyer was more accessible to the recipients of the service, both psychologically and physically. The base lawyer was the servicemen's neighborhood lawyer. To some, however, this posed a special version of client reluctance to approach a lawyer—the possibility of an enlisted man's special reluctance to consult an officer about a personal problem.

The accessibility problem has also been discussed in terms of cost savings. In recommending the rejection of the use of OEO legal services, the McCartin group also indicated that the military could meet the "needs" of the same number of clients more cheaply by using military lawyers.[57] Their arithmetic for this conclusion was essentially simple: even using a conservative case per lawyer figure, the military lawyer's pay was substantially lower than the prevailing salary of a legal service program lawyer, and the supporting staff and other overhead costs were reckoned to be lower too.

---

[54] *Id.*, sec. II, C, 6, f.

[55] *Id.*, sec. II, C, 8, c: "The Group suspects that in most cases the serviceman's problem would get lost in the shuffle, even if he could get in the door."

[56] *Id.*, sec. II, C, 6, f.

[57] *Id.*, sec. II, C, 8, b.

In sum, comparative costs, a sense of loyalty to both the military lawyer and the military client—a sense of professional identity—and feelings about control of quality and evenness of service led to a rejection of all the options and alternatives for expanded service that would have avoided converting the role of the military lawyer from one that brought no vulnerability to the legal assistance program to one that did bring vulnerability. There remains option E—the use of nonactive reservists. This option was indeed treated by the Working Group as a viable option. It still remains a viable option. Observing that there are military reserve judge advocates practicing as civilian lawyers in every state, the Working Group included in its recommendations that an expanded program use the reserve JAGs wherever possible.[58] The important thing about use of reservists, however, is that even if they were used to obviate the necessity of seeking *pro hac vice* or limited licenses for nonresident military lawyers, the role of the Staff Judge Advocates would change; they would become more active cooperators in the representation of the clients. With the reservists, the military lawyers would be more than clerks. As the Working Group observed:

> [The Reservists] could be used, with military lawyers assisting, as if they were associates, in providing full legal services, with the cooperation of courts and bar, to a limited number of personnel.[59]

The two qualifying phrases are interesting. Why the "as if" and the "with the cooperation of courts and bar"? The associate role seen is quite clearly revealed as that of courtroom participation—sitting second chair. Something more than workup is involved. But there seems to be a hesitancy, a diffidence, a sense of a new exposure—the need or the felt need for permission. Hence, the tentative "as if" and the felt need for bar approval and cooperation as well as court approval. The McCartin Group reviewed the *pro hac vice* rules; most states allowed the courts to admit nonresident counsel for particular matters when a member of the local bar was associated as counsel and was the responsible party on the pleadings.[60] Insofar as the additional counsel duties military lawyers performed out of court were in cases where they associated with civilian lawyers—albeit reservists—there were no new exposures, nor were there any where the court admitted the associate military lawyer. I think that the

---

[58] *Id.*, sec. II, C, 10, b.

[59] *Id.*

[60] *Id.*, sec. II, C, 8 (b). *See also* A. KATZ, ADMISSION OF NONRESIDENT ATTORNEYS "PRO HAC VICE" (Research Contributions of the American Bar Foundation, 1968, No. 5).

concern evidenced here amounted to circumspection about possible organized bar resentment over extending the group service concept to include some selected civilian lawyers, and a feeling that even the minimally changing role of the military lawyer in such an arrangement was threatening to the bar and brought on a new vulnerability. An observation of this sensitivity is an important clue to an effect that is even more apparent when the military lawyer's role is sought to be changed to that of principal attorney of record: The military seems to attribute to the bar a veto power that is broader than its actual power, and the attribution itself creates a greater power.

The principal recommendation of the McCartin Group took this form:

> The Group recommends the use of military lawyers, or a combination of military lawyers and service employed lawyers in any expanded program, particularly when full use of the non-active duty lawyer reservists and cooperating bar members is made, to obviate, to the extent possible, the problems involved in admission to practice where assigned, and objections to the bar to the *dangers* (sic) of nonadmitted attorneys acting for the client.[61]

Other key recommendations of the McCartin Group included: (1) assignment of military lawyers to bases located in the jurisdiction of their admission, wherever practicable, and use of interservice exchange of lawyers to reduce the bar admission problem;[62] and (2) the service rendered be the widest possible, consistent with budget and the "support of the legal profession in each state and bar."[63] Suits and disputes with the command were exempted. So, too, were class actions and other elements of a "law reform" program, as were suits against the Federal Government. The program recommendations, then, envisioned a substantial shift in the role of the military lawyer. If vulnerability to bar veto were theoretically possible, the option chosen by the Group did the least to avoid it. It is doubtful, however, that the Working Group could have avoided this option. The evidence is strong that the Group was aware of the route of the greatest difficulty but felt compelled to choose it anyway:

---

[61] McCartin Report, sec. III, A, 2, i (emphasis added). The staff civilian lawyers referred to are already employed civilian lawyers. The thought of the Group was that frequently the civilian lawyer would be licensed in the jurisdiction of the base where he was employed.

[62] *Id.*, sec. III, A, 2, c and e.

[63] *Id.*, sec. III, A, 2, d. There were cutdowns here, along lines previously laid out during the time OEO programs were bidding for bar cooperation. Fee-generating matters, such as personal injury cases, were exempted from the scope of service offered.

> The Group believes that the courts and bar most readily could be per-
> suaded to accept a program which stopped short of court pleadings
> and appearances.[64]

The choice having been consciously made, the McCartin Group
turned to the political realities: (1) the need to hold the service
eligible group to nonthreatening levels, and (2) the need to "sell"
the program to the bar and bench. If approval was not needed before, but was sought, how much more dependence must have been felt
when the mechanism chosen required affirmative permission, at least
from the courts, in the form of licenses. In fact, from the language
of the Working Group and subsequent developments to implement
the pilot program, one wonders whether delivery of legal services
to clients did not become a secondary target and the licensing exercise, accompanied by the selling job, a primary objective:

> The cooperation of the state courts, the bench and the bar [is]
> vitally necessary to any expansion of the present programs. *The job
> is to sell to the bar the need, and then the extent to which the expan-
> sion should grow. The methods of implementation of allowable and
> supportable expansion can be worked out with the bar association and
> courts, once the expansion idea is accepted.*[65]

In setting the original eligibility and scope of service guidelines,
the Group went beyond setting income standards and, like the OEO,
legal aid, and other institutional programs before them, carefully
excised from the scope of service those matters which might produce
fees, such as accident cases.[66] This, too, would be a price paid for
obtaining bar cooperation.

In mapping the campaign for bar approval, the Working Group
had the benefit of opinions solicited from both the field judge advocates and from the organized civilian bar. The issues ultimately
faced by the negotiators at the local level were known to the planners; the pieces were in place. If the bar could be persuaded of the
nonthreatening aspects of serving the poverty group, the military
negotiators would still have to face a suspicion of creeping socialism.
fear that the eligibility lines would ultimately encroach on fee-
generating business. Just as important, in seeking the licenses, the
parochial feelings of the local professional societies would come into
play. Professional identification might, in the abstract, be to and
with the men of the law, but in practice it was more strongly expressed as membership in the New York bar, the California bar, and

---

[64] *Id.*, sec. II, C, 11.

[65] *Id.*, sec. II, C, 10, c (emphasis added).

[66] *Id.*, sec. II, C, 11.

the Columbus or Chicago bars. There are no national licenses. The campaign to sell the bar, therefore, takes on an even more intriguing quality. How does a single entity—the armed forces—with plans for a national law program, and a nationwide, no, worldwide, organization of lawyers go about the problem of acquiring the necessary licenses when the authority to issue the licenses is federalized? Because of unified administration and the probable reliance on out-of-state lawyers, this was unlike the problems faced in the implementation of other national law programs, such as the OEO Legal Services Program.[67]

After the McCartin Report was submitted to the Department of Defense, DOD gave tentative approval to the Group recommendations, provided that ABA "approval" could be obtained. Colonel McCartin became the negotiator for that purpose. Prior to the Annual Meeting of the ABA in St. Louis during August 1970, Colonel McCartin sent copies of the Working Group Report to the National Legal Aid and Defender Association and to several standing committees of the ABA—Legal Aid and Indigent Defendants, Legal Assistance for Servicemen, Lawyer Referral Service, Unauthorized Practice of Law, and Ethics and Professional Responsibility.[68] The issues raised in this first-round effort for national bar approval were to be raised many times over in the several negotiations with state and local bar associations:

(1) What was the level of competence of the military lawyers?

(2) Were they, or could they be, qualified to practice competently or adequately before local courts where they were stationed?

(3) Were there available or preferable alternative ways of representing the "hardship" G.I.s and their families?

(4) Was the military plan an encroachment on established mechanisms—or established expectations?

(5) Would the military lawyer be subject to discipline in a "foreign state"?

(6) Would the military lawyer provide enough continuity and stability—particularly in duty assignments—to be able to handle a going caseload at a local level? (This involved questions of court dockets, status calls, and the longevity of litigated matters.)

---

[67] Some OEO local programs had to face the issue of temporary licenses for out-of-state lawyers awaiting bar exams. *See* discussion of New Jersey and Alaska in Part II.

[68] Interview with Colonel George McCartin, May, 1971.

(7) Would the military lawyer in the service of his military clients be subject to command influence? (This is a particularly virulent version of the "problem" seen in practicing law through intermediaries.)

Although these issues were raised in the truncated negotiations between the military and the ABA committees—negotiations which lasted only two months—they were more or less abstract and muted versions of what would occur later. The ABA could not be expected to perceive the same degree of threat that several local bars would perceive when faced with pilot programs in their bailiwicks. The ABA is an amalgam of professional constituencies, speaking less for the practicing lawyers and more for overall professional interest than do the local and state bars. The ABA would have overall views on standards for the practice of law but little view on how law should in fact be practiced at the local level. Moreover, the ABA would have no say on the issuance of local licenses to practice law or on the question of *pro hac vice* admissions. It is not surprising, therefore, that the McCartin recommendations won quick approval. There was some hesitancy on the part of the Lawyer Referral Services Committee, a hesitancy based on a sense that adequate mechanisms existed for the referral of *all* comers to competent counsel, particularly those unable to pay full fees. The Standing Committee for Lawyer Referral Services ultimately gave its approval, as did the other committees that were approached. It must be kept in mind, however, that the main threat to the bar had been removed before negotiations were commenced. The program was "sold" as a poverty legal service program. This enabled the ABA to approach the issue as "settled" in advance on the major question of approving a group legal service program. The historical paradox was operating: bar approval of the group delivery of legal services where the beneficiaries could not pay—such as OEO and legal aid—and bar disapproval of group legal services where the beneficiaries could pay.

The ABA Standing Committee on Ethics and Professional Responsibility issued an Informal Opinion covering the expanded military legal assistance program on August 9, 1971.[69] The opinion, which found no ethical objections to the expanded program, is interesting in terms of its coverage. The Committee found it had no jurisdiction over the two central questions raised by the military: Did the program have to be limited to "hardship" cases? And should

---

[69] ABA Comm. on Ethics and Professional Responsibility, Informal Opinion No. 1166 (1970).

27

military lawyers have access to civilian courts? The opinion (Informal Opinion 1166) said:

> Apart from the general concept of expansion of service, the two areas of expansion which you seemed to urge particularly in your [Colonel McCartin's] letter were (1) availability of more complete legal services to members of the armed forces and their families who are *not* living at the poverty level (or "extreme hardship cases"); and (2) access of military lawyers to the courts.
>
> Neither of these two questions raises any question within our jurisdiction. *Whatever may be the views of this Committee, the question of limitation of OEO legal services benefits to extreme hardship cases in the military family is one to be resolved by Congress.* Access to the courts of the several states is a matter determined by the law of each state, and access to the federal courts is likewise a question of law. Questions of law are not within our scope.[70]

The Committee finding of absence of jurisdiction over the question of who should be eligible for services offered through legal service programs—in this instance military legal assistance offices—is indeed puzzling, particularly in view of the "observations" that it then offers to "guide [the military's] expansion of services." The Committee Cited both DR–103 (D)(3) and DR 2–104(A)(3) to support the propositions that a lawyer "may cooperate in a dignified manner with the legal activities of a 'military legal assistance office' provided his independent judgment is exercised on behalf of his client without interference or control by any organization"; and that a lawyer who is furnished or paid by "a military legal assistance office" may represent a member or beneficiary thereof to the extent prescribed."[71] The Committee went on to observe that the extent of the group implied by the explicit coverage of "military legal assistance programs" in the Code of Professional Responsibility is "only . . . members of the military or their families."[72]

What the Committee seems to be doing, rather than finding "no jurisdiction," is registering dismay over the accidentally settled nature of the issues. There certainly is jurisdiction. By exempting "military legal assistance programs" from the strictures against the group offering of legal services and the third party payment for those services—and without any income test—the Code of Professional Responsibility had essentially provided that cooperation with such a program was ethical regardless whether the program was restricted to those servicemen or their families who could not afford

---

[70] *Id.*, at 1 (emphasis added).

[71] *Id.* at 1–2.

[72] *Id.* at 2.

to pay. To be sure, when the Code was written, the military legal assistance program looked to be limited to incidental service coupled with a lawyer referral service. There was, at the time the Code was drafted, no indication of possible expansion to full services to all military across the board. The Committee's "feelings" are then expressed in their guiding observations:

> EC 2–16 provides that ". . . reasonable fees should be charged in appropriate cases to clients able to pay for them." . . . *Accordingly, where a member of the military or his family is able to pay a reasonable fee for the desired legal services, the matter should be referred to a lawyer in private practice and not handled by the military legal assistance office at public expense.*[73]

Does the Committee's conclusion follow correctly from EC 2–16? Or from their opening remarks that the eligibility criteria are a matter for Congress? Moreover, doesn't the exemption of military legal assistance programs in DR 2–103(d)(3) and DR 2–104 (A)(3) mean that if Congress or the military choose to provide services even for those who can afford to pay for them it would automatically *not* be "an appropriate case" for the client to pay his own fee? The committee placed its own moral judgment on the question of socialized delivery of legal services. The Committee's difficulty and their puzzling denial of jurisdiction may have been forced by a realization that, at the time, over 20 states had already adopted the Code of Professional Responsibility.

The Committee suggested two other guidelines to the military. It cited EC 2–30 ("employment should not be accepted by a lawyer when he is unable to render competent service").[74] The issue of competence was asserted or inferred throughout the several negotiations with local and state bar associations. Was the military lawyer competent to represent his clients? The Committee also returned to DR 2–103(D) (a lawyer shall exercise "independent professional judgement") as a way of saying: Beware of command influence.[75]

What may be more puzzling than the Committee's treatment of its jurisdiction coupled with its willingness to "suggest" about the ethics of payment and the like—was the military's quest for an opinion on how far beyond "hardship" their program could go. This is puzzling in view of the McCartin Report's circumspection about

---

[73] *Id.* at 2 (emphasis added).

[74] *Id.* at 2. Incorrectly cited by Committee as EC 2–3. Why the committee did not cite DR 6–101 for the same proposition raises an interesting question. That section makes it a disciplinary offense for a lawyer to handle a matter where he is not competent.

[75] *Id.* at 3.

the political difficulties anticipated beyond the borders of poverty and in view of the fact that the actual request for program approval, at the time, was tied into OEO standards. At least that is the impression the military was seeking to convey. The puzzle can be understood if one remembers the military's own internal discomfort about splitting the group and if one looks more closely at the guidelines ultimately issued by the Department of Defense. As we shall see presently and more fully, the guidelines for eligibility under the expanded program were quite distinct from the guidelines for OEO legal services.

On August 13, 1970 the Board of Governors of the ABA approved the experimental expansion of the military legal assistance program.[76] The approval was for "pilot" or "test programs" in "such states as cooperate and agree with the objectives of *giving* complete legal service" in military personnel "subject to such limitations as to which the Department of Defense and the states and civilian bar associations may agree." [77] The ABA resolution provided that the data from the pilot programs be made available for evaluation to the ABA, the OEO, and the Department of Defense. The nature of the quick "approval" in some ways validates the military assumption in seeking it. Nothing was lost. But was anything gained? What was endorsed by the ABA was an experiment—that is all that the military requested and all that it would continue to request at the local level as part of the "sell." The ABA, in essence, approved an experiment which needed local implementation. In one way, then, the American Bar Association "approval" was like the encouragement given by the man who discovered his wife and a wildcat in a fight for survival—"go wife! go wildcat!" It has a posture of waiting to see what would happen; whether there were states which would "agree with the objectives of *giving* complete legal service" (third party payment), and would "cooperate"; and observing the form and scope of the limitations which would be applied. The selection of the term "giving" in the ABA Resolution is interesting and revealing. One questions whether the distribution of a fringe benefit in lieu of cash payment is ever "giving." The characterization is both incorrect and gratuitous.

The stage was set for the attempted implementation of the expanded program. It is here that the core of our study begins. The data principally relate to the ways in which the military and the local bars and courts went about reaching an accommodation or

---

[76] For text of ABA Resolution, *see* text at Note 6, *supra*.

[77] ABA Board of Governors. Proceedings. August 1970 (emphasis added).

arriving at an impasse; the issues raised, settled, avoided, or found remaining; and the ways that the parties related to the power of granting or withholding access to civilian courts.[78] The next section deals more specifically with bar action and reaction.

II. LOCAL IMPLEMENTATION OF THE PILOT PROGRAM

The directive for the implementation of pilot programs and the accompanying guidelines issued on October 26, 1970 by the Office of the Secretary of Defense to the Secretaries of the various Armed Forces gave considerable flexibility to each military service to shape its own approach and its own experiment.[79] The key Guideline read:

> Standards of eligibility for expanded legal services should be coordinated between the military departments but *such standards do not necessarily have to be identical for test purposes.* The basic standard of eligibility is that the *recipient of legal services is unable to pay a fee* to a civilian lawyer *for the services involved without substantial hardship to himself or his family.*[80]

The "basic standard" was anything but an OEO or a poverty standard. It may, in fact, for some or most of the problems that people take to lawyers, be more descriptive of the situation facing a majority of the population.[81] Legal costs, in other than the preventive mode, are viewed by significant segments of the population as "catastrophic," likely to cause "substantial hardship."

Was the Office of the Secretary of Defense evidencing the same ambivalence here about tying the standards for expanded legal services to a poverty test as had been evidenced throughout the study by the McCartin Group and as had been evidenced to the question posed to the ABA Committee on Ethics and Professional Responsibility? Since the military was in the process of seeking a dramatic pay

---

[78] The data were gathered by the author in numerous field trips. I was granted access to all documents pertaining to negotiations about the pilot program by the Judge Advocates of the Army, Navy, Coast Guard, Air Force, and Marine Corps in Washington in July 1971. In addition, local military and local bar and court people were interviewed and specific local material was gathered—between May 4, 1971 and October 28, 1971—in San Diego, Cal.; Fort Monmouth, N.J.; Denver, Colo.; Shreveport, La.; Fort Riley, Kan.; Pearl Harbor and Honolulu, Hawaii; Elmendorf Air Force Base and Anchorage, Alas.; Richards-Gebaur Air Force Base, Mo.; Pensacola and Tallahasee, Fla.; and Camp Lejeune and Jacksonville, N.C. I attended two meetings of the ABA Standing Committee on Legal Assistance for Servicemen (Chairman Louis M. Brown was kind enough to invite me) May 3 and 4, 1971 and November 15–17, 1971.

[79] *See* note 1, *supra.*

[80] *See* note 7, *supra*, Guideline 3 (emphasis added).

[81] *See* B. CHRISTENSEN, LAWYERS FOR PEOPLE OF MODERATE MEANS (1970).

raise which would have the effect of placing all military personnel and their careers above the poverty line,[82] was the "basic standard" a way out of the political dilemma posed by the need to sell the experimental program to the civilian bar, on the one hand—assuring the civilian bar that there would be no loss of income—and the internal need to expand the legal services program to everyone, on the other hand? There was a double message: "Get the cooperation of the bar, do what you have to, but see that the program is implemented, because its importance transcends intramural eligibility standards (which in the long-run are going to be uncomfortable anyway)." The military departments, in their "selling job," did use some differential standards—the Navy used an overall E-3 and below standard, the Army used an E-4 cutoff, and in some specific negotiations even more stringent eligibility standards were set.

The other part of the "sell"—and its application—is probably more important. Although the directive for the Department of Defense was silent on the method of implementing, all of the military departments, through the implementing directions of the Judge Advocates General, adopted the gloss of the McCartin Report. The Command and Staff Judge Advocates at the bases where a pilot program was planned (who were given the actual responsibility of seeking to implement the program) were instructed to obtain "agreements" and "understandings" from the local bar.[83] The Navy instructed its staff judge advocates to enter into written agreements with the local bar and the courts.[84] Only the Coast Guard, which is not a military department—it is under the Department of Transportation—did not require agreement with the local bars, but only "contact" with them "to obtain insofar as possible their support."[85] In addition to bar approval, the implementing directives in some instances asked that the approval of the courts be obtained, a conceptual approval that went beyond the implicit approval which would follow from the issuance of licenses or the amendments to rules.

---

[82] The pay raise did in fact ensue, and, although temporarily caught in the wage-price freeze, it took effect November 15, 1971.

[83] The Military Departments issued their own guidelines to the staff judge advocates: Air Force, October 14, 1970; Navy, December 8, 1970; Army, January 4, 1971.

[84] Navy Guidelines, Guideline 1. The agreements did not have to be formal, but they had to be reduced to writing.

[85] Commandant, U.S. Coast Guard, to Commanders First and Third Coast Guard Districts, December 3, 1970, re: Establishment of Pilot Legal Assistance Program, at 2; and U.S. Coast Guard, General Guidelines for Legal Assistance Pilot Programs, Guideline 1.

As has been observed, the very act of arrogating to the bar and the bench an absolute power of veto over the expansion of the military legal services program may have created a more extensive power than existed in reality. We will be able to observe the effects of this strategy as we follow the specific negotiations. At the time that the implementing directives were issued, however, a "warning" was issued by Howard C. Westwood, a member of the Executive Committee of the National Legal Aid and Defender Association, who had been asked to comment on the Air Force and Navy Legal Assistance Guidelines. He said, in part:

> [T]here is a concept of securing "permission" from state and local bar associations. This is naive. . . . It is quite impractical and wrong for there to be a nationally adopted edict that there must be *permission* from underdefined "state and local bar associations" for essential elements in the pilot projects.
>
> Fifty years or more of legal aid experience teach that sometimes it is indispensible to proceed with a legal aid project even in the face of opposition from *some* bar association. And it would be all but absurd absolutely to require affirmative approval in all instances. . . . The requirement of agreement with "state and local bar associations" is entirely too unqualified and is dangerous. Nor is it clear that in all instances approval "by the local courts" would be necessary on all aspects. . . .[86]

Westwood also observed that where licenses for out-of-state lawyers were needed bar approval might be necessary.

The Westwood comments not only question the military guidelines but also, by implication, raise questions about the form of the ABA Resolution which seemed to compel assent, approval, and cooperation by the state and local bar associations as a condition—subsequent—of ABA approval. In any event, warnings aside, the quest for bar "approval" was the dominant mode used by staff judge advocates in local negotiations. The pure conception of the pilot program called for licenses for nonresident lawyers. The military's view was that bar approval for this was necessary. We shall see that in instances where bar approval was not obtained—or was not as extensive as sought—most frequently the military tailored its program to match the extent of the "approval." This frequently meant that the idea of securing licenses for nonresident attorneys was abandoned.

The approach of and the results obtained by the United States

---

[86] Howard C. Westwood, Tentative Comments on Air Force and Navy Legal Assistance Guidelines, at 3 and 7.

Coast Guard in its efforts to implement the pilot program were exceptional. Perhaps this was due to its abandonment of the need for "approval" from the bar; perhaps it was due to the personalities of the staff judge advocates; or perhaps it was due to the nature of the locales, regions, and jurisdictions where the Coast Guard sought to implement the program. At any rate, the experience was different It is here, then, where we will pick up our examination of the military lawyers, civilian courts, and the organized bar.[87]

The Coast Guard chose to implement the pilot program in the First and Third Coast Guard Districts, headquartered in Boston and New York, respectively. Because of its size, the uniqueness of its mission, and the dispersion of its personnel, the Coast Guard approached the expanded program on a regional—District Headquarter—basis, attempting to give its legal officers as much flexibility as possible. The Coast Guard has a strength of only 40,000. It has more law enforcement and marine safety functions than it has armed service functions. There are no heavy concentrations of troops in any single locale. There are few lawyers. Accordingly, if the Coast Guard was going to offer more complete legal services to its personnel, it would have to rely on lawyers from the strictly military departments to supplement the efforts of Coast Guard lawyers. Accordingly, the Coast Guard undertook to obtain broad geographical approval of the pilot program in the regions of its two selected District headquarters—Boston and New York.

To conserve its manpower, the Coast Guard guidelines limited court representation to misdemeanors on the criminal side and excluded divorce from the civil side. For felonies and divorce, however, permission was extended for "in office" work where deemed "necessary or desirable."[88]

The Legal Assistance Officer for the First Coast Guard District

---

[87] Considerable attention was given to the question of whether the names of places, jurisdictions, and people discussed in Part II should be disguised. I felt that this was intellectually unsound: Disguises are frequently too thin if important material is included. Moreover, the geography, the character of the communities, the nature of the local bars, the local laws and rules, and the community-bar-military relations are all important parts of the study. Beyond that, the observations made frequently require citation to unpublished but available reports, memoranda, and letters. The reader is entitled to these data for purposes of critically evaluating the matters presented. By openly citing the material I rest part of the dialogue which may ensue properly on those who would suggest its inaccuracies. By "blinding" the study, the facts would remain forever as I saw them. If this article in a few places takes on characteristics of an exposé, it is because the events and exchanges reported give it this character.

[88] U.S. Coast Guard, General Guidelines for Legal Assistance Pilot Programs, Guideline 4.

in Boston—Commander J. V. Flanagan—accepted the latitude given to him by the Coast Guard directive. He made no direct formal request of any bar association, but only made informal contact "to obtain insofar as possible their support." Commander Flanagan reserved his formal approaches for the courts. The approach was direct and simple:

> Here is what we are going to do. Give us the necessary tools.

The results were likewise direct, simple and fast.

Massachusetts: On February 19, 1971 the Coast Guard formally filed a request for limited licenses with the Clerk of the Supreme Judicial Court for the Commonwealth of Massachusetts. Prior to that time Commander Flanagan made informal contacts with members of the Massachusetts bar. He was informed that the pilot program would not threaten most lawyers practicing but that a formal debate within the bar associations would stir up the sense of displacement already felt by some lawyers after Massachusetts became the first state to adopt a no-fault automobile liability rule.

On March 1, 1971 the Massachusetts Supreme Court entered the following order:

1. Until the further order of this court, a member of the bar of any State, or of the District of Columbia, on active duty with any one of the armed services, may appear in any court of the Commonwealth with the written authorization (which may be general and not confined to a particular case) of the senior legal officer of such service on active duty within the service district which includes the Commonwealth, to represent in civil or criminal causes junior noncommissioned officers and enlisted personnel of such service who might not otherwise be able to afford proper legal assistance. A copy of each such written authorization shall be filed by the senior legal officer with the Clerk of the Supreme Judicial Court for Suffolk County [Boston].
2. [Copies of orders to be sent to chief judges and clerks of all inferior courts in the Commonwealth.] [89]

A model order. And a model "negotiation." There are few of these. The eligibility criteria is the basic standard and not pegged to the difficult to define OEO standard. The license to practice is general for the clientele in question. And future permission depends only upon the administrative decisions of senior legal officers responsible for servicing the clients.

In contrast to the Coast Guard approach, one should consider the

---

[89] In the Matter of Legal Assistance for Certain Members of the Armed Services, Supreme Judicial Court for the Commonwealth of Massachusetts, March 1, 1971.

Navy's position about implementing their own pilot program in Massachusetts even *after* the March 1, 1971 order, which was not restricted to the Coast Guard, had been entered. The Navy directive required written agreements with the local bars. Because of this directive, notwithstanding the permission extended by the Massachusetts Supreme Court, the Navy's approach was gingerly. The District Legal Officer informed Washington on May 4, 1971 that it would "open negotiations with the local civilian bar," but that:

> [I]t will be delicate, inasmuch as the no-fault insurance law in Massachusetts has severely dented the local attorneys' incomes and we envision that they will not give up any potential business gracefully.[90]

For reasons of comity—growing out of either a more visible presence than the Coast Guard or the Navy lawyer's membership in two brotherhoods—or reasons of administrative inertia, the Navy stood ready to render homage to the local bar, even *after* the primary reason for doing so had been removed by the Court. Unlike the Coast Guard, the Navy appeared to be willing to render unto Caesar more than that which was Caesar's.

Rhode Island: The approach and the result in Rhode Island was the same as Massachusetts. After the Massachusetts success, Commander Flanagan merely made application directly to the Supreme Court of Rhode Island. There is no indication of "negotiations" with the Rhode Island Bar Association. The Rhode Island Supreme Court entered the *same* order as did the Massachusetts Court.[91]

The Navy in Rhode Island had thoughts of implementing a pilot program at Newport after the order was entered. It found the local (Newport County) bar "not happy with the Supreme Court order," willing to be "appeased" somewhat by the eligibility criteria, but still sensing their "bread and butter" was involved.[92]

New Hampshire: New Hampshire surprised everyone, even the success-laden Coast Guard. Pursuing the same course as Massachusetts and Rhode Island, Commander Flanagan wrote to the Clerk

---

[90] Report from First Naval District Legal Offices to Commander Robert Redding, May 4, 1971.

[91] *In re:* the Matter of Legal Assistance for Certain Members of the Armed Forces, Supreme Court of Rhode Island, No. 1380 M.P., April 6, 1971. Note also that the Supreme Court of Iowa has entered a Massachusetts-Rhode Island type of order with no application from the military.

[92] Report from Staff Judge Advocate, Newport to Judge Advocate General, United States Navy, June 9, 1971. The staff judge advocate also reported that the Newport County Bar Association had been and was opposed to OEO Legal Service Programs.

of the New Hampshire Supreme Court and received a reply that any order of court was unnecessary—redundant—in view of Section 311:1 of the New Hampshire Revised Statutes, which provided:

> A party in any cause or proceeding may appear, plead, prosecute or defend, in his proper person or *by any citizen* of good character.[93]

In other words, if military personnel wanted to be represented by military lawyers, that was their choice and consonant with public policy in the state. That is not to say that New Hampshire does not have an unauthorized practice of the law concept. They do. Section 311:7 provides that no person shall be "permitted to commonly practice as an attorney in court" unless he has been admitted to practice by the Court.[94] There are also provisions for holding out to the public as a lawyer.[95] And, as of 1968, New Hampshire was trying a three-year unified bar experiment, where in order to practice law in New Hampshire an attorney had to be a dues paying member of the New Hampshire Bar Association.[96]

The Clerk's response—surely with the assent of the New Hampshire Supreme Court—is doubly interesting in view of the unauthorized practice rules and the unified bar experiment. A distinction seems to be drawn between holding out to the public as a lawyer and serving the defined needs of a defined group—albeit self-defined. This is indeed a rare model for an approach to unauthorized practice of law.

Maine: No one's record is perfect. Commander Flanagan did run into problems in Maine. It is not altogether clear whether it was court or bar originated, but a very limited order was entered by the Maine Supreme Court allowing military lawyers to appear for lower grade military personnel in misdemeanor cases only—no other criminal cases and no civil cases.[97] The issue raised was concern over the quality and competence of representation by judge advocates in complex matters, particularly matters which might pose a problem of continuity of counsel if the lawyer in charge of the case were transferred from his duty station while the matter was pending. This, of course, is a real concern. It is a problem not faced by the

---

[93] NEW HAMPSHIRE REVISED STATUTES (1966, with 1971 Pocket parts) sec. 311:1.

[94] *Id.*, sec. 311:7.

[95] *Id.*, secs. 311:7a thru 311:7f.

[96] *In re* Unification of New Hampshire Bar, 109 N.H. 260, 248 A.2d 709 (1968). The New Hampshire Supreme Court as part of its inherent jurisdiction, adopted the trial unification rule.

[97] Order of Supreme Court of Maine, September 23, 1971.

legal aid offices and OEO legal services programs, because there is an assumed stability of assignments. One commentator has observed that military lawyer assignments—two to four years—are as stable as OEO legal services lawyer tenures. It is a problem that the bench and bar properly raise, and one which needs attention from the program planners. An alternative approach to a uniform rule, however, is both an application of and a modification of the rule about not accepting employment in cases where competent representation cannot be given: "Don't start anything you can't finish." But the limitation, as with most professional standards, is capable of self-application and self-limitation and does not need to be translated into admissions standards.

The Coast Guard and the Maine State Bar Association and local bars have worked out a cooperative arrangement for the excluded cases. They will be referred, as under the old legal assistance program; the local lawyers will be chief counsel and the military lawyers will be associate counsel.

New York: The First Coast Guard District in New York City has only approached one jurisdiction—the state of New York. Even this may not have been necessary, because the Coast Guard had been satisfied with the representation afforded its personnel by the Legal Aid Society of New York City. Pursuant to the Department of Defense Guideline—advisory only as to the Coast Guard—the Coast Guard intended to maintain a working relationship with Legal Aid.[98] The Coast Guard lawyers would conduct interviews and investigations, and prepare working papers, including pleadings, motions, and briefs, and the Legal Aid lawyers would make the court appearances. Coast Guard lawyers in court cases would, where permitted, act as associate counsel.

The Coast Guard sought a Massachusetts-type order from the New York Court of Appeals. The Court declined to change its admission rules but did explain its reasons to the Coast Guard. Associate Judge Adrian Burke called the District Legal Office and explained the Court's hesitancy to amend the admissions rule: (1) New York has a liberal *pro hac vice* admission rule, which, although discretionary with the trial courts, seldom results in petitions for *pro hac vice* being denied. (2) The Court felt that generally the Coast Guard would have at least one member of the New York bar assigned to the Third District Legal Office, and that "attorneys from other juris-

---

[98] Interview with Captain Henry A. Cretella, Washington, D.C., March 9 and July 8, 1971. *See* DOD Guideline 4 (note 7 *supra*) and note 4 *supra*.

dictions could, as is customarily done in New York law firms, sign papers, pleadings and motions in the name of the New York attorney appearing thereon.[99] We shall see the particular formula advanced in reason (2) followed in many instances in other jurisdictions: Notice is taken of the active role of the military legal assistance officer. He is allowed to function as counsel but not as counsel of record, and no formal action is taken with respect to his status. From the military's viewpoint there is an affirmative and a negative element. The out-of-state counsel is able to resolve conflicts by negotiation, as long as access to the courts is available. This remains the single most important program advance; a legal service program would indeed be in trouble if it needed to litigate a large percentage of its caseload. On the negative side, where the associate counsel formula is followed, the assignment of lawyers is limited by the external demand that at least one judge advocate assigned to duty be licensed in the jurisdiction—unless either cooperating reservists or other civilian counsel are used.

The Chief Judge of the New York Court of Appeals circulated to all members of the state judiciary a memorandum noting the nature of the expanded legal service program—"the armed services intend to supply legal counsel, in civil or criminal cases to junior noncommissioned officer and enlisted personnel who might not otherwise be able to afford proper legal assistance" (again the basic test!) —and called the judges attention to the rule and the liberal *pro hac vice* policy.[100] This memorandum had the effect of endorsing the pilot program and advancing the implementation, even though, for the most part, the Coast Guard lawyers would continue to cooperate with Legal Aid for court cases. Their role was now legitimated.

In large measure the Coast Guard "success" in obtaining broad orders was due to a direct approach made to courts. The courts, however, are all centered in the Northeast and may be idiosyncratic in their liberal attitude about group legal service, poverty law, and the issuance of either special licenses or the admission of nonresident lawyers *pro hac vice*. Also the organized bar raised few objections. Certainly the low visibility of the Coast Guard contributed to the successful implementation of the pilot programs. The Coast Guard recognized this and studiously avoided any public relations campaign

---

[99] Memorandum from Third Coast Guard District Legal Office to Commandant, May 11, 1971.

[100] *See* 29 CONSOLIDATED LAWS OF NEW YORK ANNOTATED 372 [Court of Appeals Rules for Admission of Attorneys and Counselors-at-Law, Rule VII–4] (McKinney 1968) ; *see also* Spanos v. Skouras Theatres Corp., 364 F.2d 161 (2d. Cir. 1966).

about the program or even about the fact of the favorable court orders or directives. When the Coast Guard lawyers appeared in court under one of the permissive orders or rules the fact "wasn't flaunted." [101] Beyond that, the Coast Guard practice was in big cities —Boston, Portsmouth, New York—which contributed to the program's relative invisibility. As we leave the quiet precincts of the Coast Guard and the Northeast we see that most of the other implementing negotiations did not go as smoothly.

The United States Army had a relatively easy time implementing the program at Forts Monmouth and Dix in New Jersey. But it was unexpected.[102] Contact was made with the Burlington County (Fort Dix) and Monmouth County (Fort Monmouth) Bar Associations. Both bars approved the program of service limited to the lower income troops and their dependents.[103] Both bars suggested that the state bar association be approached. This was done through a reserve judge advocate. (In New Jersey, as elsewhere, wherever possible, contact with bar groups—and courts—was made through reserve judge advocates, pursuant to the suggestions of the McCartin Report and the Department of Defense.) The Trustees of the New Jersey State Bar were approached at a regular meeting—in the Bahamas—and seemed to have been impressed by the ABA endorsement of the program. They, too, endorsed the program as limited to E–4 and below.[104] In a way, since the practice was going to be conducted in two counties where the local bars had already approved the pilot program, the State Bar endorsement was as free and abstract as the ABA endorsement—perhaps even more free, because a mechanism already existed in New Jersey for implementing the pilot program without bar approval, an existing court rule covering out-of-state lawyers employed by legal service programs.[105]

Before discussing that rule, however, it would be well here to relate the insight gained from discussion with several of the Army negotiators in New Jersey as to why they sought bar permission, even when it wasn't necessary. It was explained first as politeness, but then in

---

[101] Interview with Captain Henry A. Cretella, July 8, 1971.

[102] Interview with Colonel John Zalonis, July 9, 1971.

[103] The data here were derived from several interviews conducted at Fort Monmouth at a conference attended by the civilian and military bars in May 1971. The author is particularly indebted to Captain Elliot H. Vernon, the officer in charge of the Fort Monmouth pilot program and the New Jersey admitted supervising attorney for that office.

[104] The President of the New Jersey State Bar told the author that approval would not have been given if the program had covered those who could pay.

[105] N.J.R. 1:21–3(d).

terms of comfort in style, of working through a chain of command—from bottom to top—just as is done in the Army. The Staff Judge Advocate at Fort Monmouth explained that they didn't want to "ram the program down anyone's throat." Upon analysis, though, it appears that the policy was dictated by the fact that the Army felt more visible at Forts Monmouth and Dix among smaller units of population and practicing lawyers. Whether the pilot program worked or not, they wanted to get along with the community—it was a matter of comity. Beyond Monmouth and Dix, this may have also shaped the Department directives, particularly for those services and at the particular posts that had a continuing problem of community relations. And now back to the court rule covering legal services programs.

Rule 1:21–3(d) of the New Jersey Supreme Court rules provides:

A graduate of an approved law school who is a member of the bar of another state or of the District of Columbia and employed by or is associated with a legal services program approved by the Director of Legal Services, Department of Community Affairs shall be permitted to practice, under the supervision of a member of the bar of this State before all courts of this State on all causes in which he is associated with such legal services program, subject to the following conditions:

(1) Permission . . . shall become effective [when evidence of graduation, membership in out of state bar (in good standing), and statement signed by Director of Legal Services (State) that attorney is employed in an approved program.]

(2) [Permission ceases when employment by program ceases.]

(3) [Notice of cessation of employment.]

(4) Permission to practice in this State under this rule shall remain in effect no longer than 2½ years;

(5) [Permission may be revoked or suspended at any time.]

(6) Out of state attorneys permitted to practice under this rule are not, and shall not represent themselves to be, members of the bar of this State.[106]

With this rule, the Army's implementation was simple: Have the State Director of Legal Services, Department of Community Affairs, approve the pilot program. The Director, Carl Bianchi, was extremely cooperative, and the Army program was certified by his office as "an approved legal service program." For the Army, with a post the size of Fort Monmouth, the requirement that a New Jersey

---

[106] *Id.* The effective date of the Rule was July 1, 1970. The beginning sections of Rule 1:21–3 (a) thru (c), adopted earlier, relate to a similar model: allowing law students to practice before the courts in limited kinds of matters and under "supervision" of admitted attorneys and through the auspices of legal service programs. This can be seen in terms of the students' education. But it also can be seen in terms of delivering more legal service to those who need it.

lawyer "supervise" the caseload did not appear to be too burdensome. The number of lawyers assigned to Fort Monmouth is usually large. At least one lawyer from populous New Jersey can be found. Let us, however, examine the requirement from the perspective of the bar and the bench: Why is this model of supervision or responsibility by a locally admitted attorney (followed in varying forms elsewhere) deemed necessary or desirable?

The reasons generally assigned for having supervision by responsible locally admitted lawyers have to do with either protecting the client or protecting the integrity of the legal process. The reasons frequently rest on assumptions subsumed in the act of licensing lawyers in the first place. Two major reasons advanced—familiarity with local procedures and local rules of practice and amenability to court supervision of quality as well as process—are reasons which can sound both in terms of client protection and in terms of protecting the smooth operation of the judicial process. They are also reasons which can sound in terms of protection of those already admitted to practice in a jurisdiction—protecting the monopoly granted by the license. (The general arguments may be far less convincing in terms of public protection than the specific argument about continuity of representation—raised in Maine. That is an argument which runs to loyalty and commitment.) In terms of client protection and protection of judicial supervision over the bar, the standards are no better as applied to out-of-state attorneys than the level of standards realistically imposed and supervision actually imposed on locally admitted attorneys. Clients are ill served if they are represented by lawyers unfamiliar with either what they *are* doing or what they *should* do. What mechanisms, however, are used to assure an application of these standards to locally admitted lawyers? Clients may be ill served if they are represented by lawyers not amenable to the supervision or disciplinary processes of the courts before which they practice. What is the reality of supervision and discipline over locally admitted lawyers? A realistic assessment of these issues requires a dismal response: Damned little is done to assure quality representation by members of any local bar. Advancement of arguments and the incorporation of a standard calling for "supervision" by local lawyers are, unless the local attorneys are themselves supervised, disingenuous.

This is not to say that the reasons lack merit. We need mechanisms for assuring quality representation, court readiness, and professional scrutiny of performance. Too little real attention is paid to issues of competence. What is suggested here is that a double standard is involved. Issues about competence are raised in questioning those outside but not those inside the club. It may be that the double standard was born of the local licensing process, itself, and the ensuing parochialism. Beyond that, however, the double standard fails to take into account some of the realities of legal education and legal practice. There are more similarities in the practice than dissimilarities when passing from locality to locality or from state to state. National standards are involved and are ignored. The perpetuation of fragmented standards bears close examination. What is suggested is that local licensing arguments may inhibit—by soothing—the search for national standards and national scrutiny.

The paradox of the "supervision" or "responsible" local attorney rule is that attorneys senior in service and more seasoned in terms of competence, by virtue of the accidents of their licensing and duty assignments, can be supervised by less able lawyers.

The Air Force ran into three variants of the supervision or principal counsel rule—as a result of the negotiations in Missouri, Illinois, and Louisiana. Unlike the New Jersey rule, however, the experience in these states did not provide for across-the-board special admission of nonresident military lawyers. They allowed them to assist counsel of record—locally admitted lawyers. But, unlike most *pro hac vice* rules, these jurisdictions did not allow nonresident counsel to take a primary responsibility.[107]

Missouri: [108] Richards-Gebaur Air Force Base and Headquarters Air Force Communications Service, at that base—located on the southern end of Kansas City, Missouri—were selected by the Air Force as a pilot program site. Approach was made to the Missouri Bar Administration Advisory Committee through a reserve judge advocate—a circuit judge. This agency, which reports directly to the Missouri Supreme Court, has supervisory powers over the Missouri Bar, which is an integrated bar. Aside from its disciplinary functions, the Missouri Bar Administration acts as a superbar agency in the consideration of court rule changes that affect the integrated bar rules. In this capacity they act as initiators and advisors. Colonel Joseph Lowry, Staff Judge Advocate for the Communications Serv-

---

[107] There are generally requirements that local counsel must be of record in rules for the admission of nonresident attorneys *pro hac vice*. There are, at least, reasons that relate to continuity of service to the client and availability, in the jurisdiction, for the acceptance of service of papers and the making of appearances for motions and status calls. Rarely do *pro hac vice* rules require that principal responsibility rest with local counsel. *See* KATZ, note 60 *supra*.

[108] The data here came from interviews with Fred Hulse, Chairman, Advisory Committee, Missouri Bar Administration; judge advocates at Richards-Gebaur; and several members of the Missouri bar.

ice, appeared before the Missouri Bar Administration Advisory Committee in January 1971 and outlined the pilot program. It is not clear whether Colonel Lowry initially asked for, or intended to ask for, a rule allowing the admission of nonresident lawyers on an across-the-board basis as in Massachusetts. From the discussion with the Advisory Committee, however, it is clear that the operation that Colonel Lowry ultimately described called for the "supervision" of all court cases by a Missouri lawyer on his staff. The Missouri lawyer would sign all pleadings and make all court appearances, requesting *pro hac vice* admission of out-of-state counsel where administratively desirable from the program's viewpoint. The nonresident lawyers would assist the Missouri lawyer. This ducked the hard question and left his request for approval of the pilot program as a request for general "approval" coupled with a "finding" that unauthorized practice of the law was not involved where nonresident laywers interviewed clients, worked on matters in the office, and "assisted" Missouri counsel in court. And that is what he got: general approval. The Minute adopted by the Advisory Committee stated:

> The Committee conferred with Colonel Joseph R. Lowry, USAF, Staff Judge Advocate at Richards-Gebaur Air Force Base in western Missouri in reference to the establishment of a Pilot Legal Assistance Program at said base. Colonel Lowry presented the method of operation of the pilot program in which Judge Advocate lawyers at the air base would represent needy *airmen* who had incomes of less than $3,000 and if civilians would qualify for legal assistance as provided by the Office of Economic Opportunity.
>
> The Committee gave careful consideration to the Matter and at the conclusion of its conference with Colonel Lowry it was the unanimous opinion of the Committee that no problems had been presented which might involve unauthorized practice of law by lawyers from other states *in the event the program was followed as presented* by Colonel Lowry.[109]

The avowed intent to use Missouri lawyers in a supervisory capacity, then, became part of the gloss of the understanding.

The fixed dollar eligibility standards—$3,000 limit—set by the Advisory Committee were unsatisfactory to Colonel Lowry and he suggested an amendment to the Minute:

> [T]he Air Base would represent needy *military* personnel and their dependents who would otherwise meet [the OEO standards].

The pilot program, of course, called for representation of military personnel and dependents across service lines—not just airmen. And, the fixed dollar amount would be troublesome in view of Air Force

---

[109] Letter from Fred B. Hulse to Colonel Joseph Lowry, January 27, 1971 contains language of Minute (emphasis added).

guidelines.[110] What is more interesting, however, is the addition by the Committee and Colonel Lowry of the term "needy," which now joined "hardship," "extreme hardship," and "poverty" of recent vintage and bridges back to the older notions of "worthy poor." Much can be done in the name of charity.

The Richards-Gebaur program was welcomed by the local bars in the neighboring counties around Kansas City as a relief of a burden in criminal cases. Missouri has a limited public defender program for Kansas City and St. Louis and beyond that relies heavily on court appointments for indigents accused of crimes. There is no payment to appointed counsel. (The relief of the local bar can be contrasted to the hostility of the local bar in Jacksonville, North Carolina—outside of Camp Lejeune—where the State of North Carolina pays reasonable fees for the defense of indigent marines accused of crimes. This is more fully discussed below.) For criminal cases, therefore, the program was a welcome relief; judges and magistrates now appoint the judge advocates as counsel.[111] The local bar has been less sure about the program as applied to civil matters.

The judges and magistrates feel another plus from the ability to appoint military lawyers in criminal cases. They feel that the military lawyer can handle the command and red-tape problems frequently required to keep a military defendant in the jurisdiction pending trial—arranging for reassignment or detached duty. Such arrangements also facilitate release to the military in lieu of bond. Some would argue that this perceived plus from the perspective of the judges is a negative when considering the client and the lawyer-client relationship. Problems of divided loyalty are present. Command influences to keep a man in the jurisdiction may be inimical to the needs of the client. Further, the same office which defends him in the criminal case may later present the case against him in the matter of administrative discharge from the service. (These perceptions played a major role in bar opposition to the pilot program in Alaska discussed below.) This is not to say that there are not client advantages, too. The military client may feel better understood by a military lawyer.

One additional issue, considered at Richards-Gebaur and elsewhere, bears mention here. The Richards-Gebaur lawyers go into civilian courts in uniform; the Fort Monmouth lawyers do not—they wear civilian clothes. There is no fixed policy on this matter, but it is recognized that there are important symbols involved. The uniform

---

[110] Letter from Colonel Lowry to Fred Hulse, February 1, 1971.

[111] Interview with Thomas French, Magristrate for Cass County, July 30, 1971.

clearly indicates that the military takes care of its own. But, with possible hostility toward the military, does the symbol of brotherhood redound to the advantage or disadvantage of the client? There may be competing symbols. More important, what does the uniform say to the lawyer who is wearing it? Which roles is it reminding him of?

Louisiana: [112] In contrast to the initial state level approach used in Missouri, for the program at Barksdale Air Force Base, in Shreveport and Bossier City, Louisiana, the Air Force approach was more explicitly aimed at local support. It also drew on two important factors: (1) There was a history of good community-military relations; and (2) The Shreveport Bar Association had evidenced hospitality toward experimental programs—they were in the process of their own experiment with the country's first prepaid legal service plan. Letters were sent to both the Shreveport and Bossier City Bar Associations. [113] A supper meeting was arranged at the base on January 18, 1971, which was attended by the Commandant of the Second Air Force, the Staff Judge Advocate, several judge advocates, the Executive Committees of both the Shreveport and Bossier City Bar Associations and three local judges—city judges. The Staff Judge Advocate outlined the pilot program, emphasizing that it covered ratings of E–4 and below, and then frankly asked his guests for "their cooperation, advice and suggestions" for allowing military lawyers into civilian court.

The style of this approach and the approach of Colonel Lowry in Missouri exemplify an in-service dual identity paralled to, but weaker than, that of the reserve judge advocates frequently used to make contacts with the local bar and bench. The reservists belonged to the inner club—the locally admitted lawyer, the active bar member, the sitting member of the bench—and the military "call" upon them contained a suggestion that other loyalties were involved. They were reminded of a once strong, but now perhaps faint, allegiance to the military. The active-duty judge advocate has a strong allegiance to the military and an ongoing identity—at least self-identity—as a lawyer and a member of the bar somewhere. When addressing local

---

[112] Sources for these data were reports and correspondence in the files of the Legal Assistance Office, United States Air Force, Washington, D.C., and an interview with Henry A. Politz, a member of the Executive Council of the Shreveport Bar Association.

[113] Barksdale Air Force Base is located on the Bossier City side of the Red River on land that was acquired for the government by the City of Shreveport. The main economic and residential orientation of the base is toward Shreveport.

bar groups, if the correct symbols are used, the judge advocate can remind the audience that he is entitled to some degree of comity. Where the bar has failed to cooperate with the pilot program, more frequently than not the presenting judge advocate has failed to convince the bar that he is a lawyer—and that he "employs" lawyers—as well as being a military man. In fact, the judge advocates who were successful negotiators were able to convince their lawyer audiences that they were lawyers first and only incidentally military men.[114] I am not suggesting that this would be the only factor affecting either outcome or how the military lawyer is perceived: Certainly the way that a local bar relates to the issue of licensing and their own lawyerness and the way the community at large relates to the military are operating factors.

The local bar people attending the dinner at Barksdale Air Force Base suggested that questions of whether out-of-state lawyers in the program were engaged in unauthorized practice of law could be avoided entirely by having a Louisiana lawyer in the case and involved in the supervision of both case preparations and other office work. This issue was discussed and two alternatives were posed, either use Louisiana reservists or have a Louisiana lawyer assigned to Barksdale. (The latter course was followed.) The Shreveport Bar Association raised the question of appearance in uniform and asked the Air Force to further consider this issue. Two of the three judges present indicated that nonresident military lawyers would be welcome in their courts, if Louisiana lawyers were also of record—informal and continuing *pro hac vice* admission, in other words.

Both local bar associations appointed liaison members of their executive committees to continue to work with the Air Force in implementing the program. Subsequently the executive committees of both associations passed resolutions "approving" the pilot program and pledging continuing cooperation. Nonresident lawyers have appeared on behalf of servicemen in local courts. The arrangement is informal. All parties agreed that there is no way for this to happen formally without a rule change by the Louisiana Supreme Court, which in turn would involve the Ethics and Grievance Committee of the State Bar Association. The President of the Shreveport Bar Association advised the Air Force to go no further—to leave well enough alone and proceed on the basis of the informal arrange-

---

[114] The strength of the bargaining power from this dual position has been discussed, under a game theory, by Stephen Potter as the "Two Club Approach." S. POTTER, LIFEMANSHIP, OR THE ART OF GETTING AWAY WITH IT WITHOUT BEING AN ABSOLUTE PLONK (1951).

ment, there being little likelihood of approval of a rule change by the State Supreme Court.[115]

The fact that Louisiana has an integrated bar may have forced the local, informal arrangement. It also makes the local accommodation more interesting. A similar accommodation, but formal, was made locally in another integrated bar state (Texas)—for the Navy's pilot program at Corpus Christi (Nueces County). In Texas the Navy was in the process of informally approaching the State Bar. Meanwhile, the Nueces County Bar and the Navy have entered into a written agreement, approved by the local courts in the form of an order, which allowed out-of-state military lawyers to appear in court; there was no requirement that a Texas lawyer be involved. The order entered by the local court was a Massachusetts-type order. After the order was entered the President of the Texas bar suggested that the formal approach to the State Bar be omitted and that the Navy make application for an order directly to the Texas Supreme Court. He advised that leaders of the Texas bar would support the petition. Corpus Christi, like Barksdale, had enjoyed good community—military relations and like Barksdale also has a locally admitted lawyer on its staff.

Before leaving Shreveport and Barksdale, it should be noted that the primary criticism that the Shreveport Bar Association leveled at the pilot program was that its eligibility standards were too rigid, being more restrictive than the local legal aid standards. This rather relaxed attitude about the military properly extending a service to a client group should be compared to the rigid supervision of standards in places like Jacksonville, North Carolina (Camp Lejeune Marine Corps Base), discussed below, supervision reflecting fear of diversion of fee-generating matters.

Illinois: [116] The Staff Judge Advocate for the pilot program at Scott Air Force Base, at Belleville, Illinois, first approached the President of the St. Clair County Bar Association and the Chairman of the Legal Aid and Referral Committee. Historically the relations between Scott Air Force Base and the local community and bar had not been as good as those at Barksdale. Referrals under the old military LAP had been made to the private practitioners through

---

[115] A copy of the Shreveport resolution approving the plan was sent to the President of the Louisiana State Bar Association and there was an undertaking to keep the officers of the state bar informed. Letter from Robert Pugh, President of the Shreveport Bar Association to Lt. Col. Charles O'Brien, USAF, March 30, 1971.

[116] Air Force Progress Report on the Pilot Legal Assistance Program, March 9, 1971, and interview with Colonel Jerry Conner, USAF, July 7, 1971.

the Legal Aid and Referral Committee, and the chairman of that Committee was concerned, notwithstanding the pilot program's eligibility criteria, that the new program would divert fee-paying business from the bar. The Air Force offered to let the Committee handle the burden of screening interviews: This offer, which was declined, seemed to turn the negotiations around. The St. Clair County Bar Association approved the concept of the program and the eligibility criteria but not the idea of using nonresident lawyers in Illinois courts. Arrangements were made to continue to refer fee generating matters to the Lawyer Referral Committee of the St. Clair County Bar Association and to consult on borderline cases. The pilot program proceeded at Scott Air Force base using only Illinois lawyers for court appearances—one judge advocate and an Illinois civilian lawyer employed by the Air Force at Scott. Subsequently meetings were held with the local judges who gave "informal blessings" for the program. There has been no approach to the Illinois Supreme Court and only tentative approach to the Illinois State Bar Association.

As has already been suggested, when one looks closely at approvals such as those given for the Scott Air Force Base program, one is convinced that the approval was unnecessary. By using only Illinois attorneys in court, the question of whatever other services are rendered to a military clientele on federal property is beyond the jurisdiction of either the courts or the bar associations. There is nothing that needs their approval. No nonresident is asking for the use of the hall—the courts. Moreover, DR 2–103(D) of the Code of Professional Responsibility makes this even more certain—there is no unethical conduct involved in the employment of a lawyer or corporation with a military legal assistance program. This also means, however, that the Scott program is essentially the old program, with referrals in some kinds of cases made to Illinois lawyers employed by the program rather than to the civilian bar.

A pattern is faintly discernible in the Missouri, Louisiana, Illinois, and Texas negotiations. It becomes more pronounced in some jurisdictions that have either rejected the pilot program outright or have long delayed its implementation—i.e., the courts seem to await approval or consent from the bar to make changes in rules of admission. If that approval is not forthcoming or there is an evidenced bar hostility toward amending the rules of admission, the courts, too, are hesitant. It is a kind of comity, not usually spelled out, but there nevertheless. In addition, in states where there is an integrated or unified bar, the reluctance of courts to act without bar approval seems greater. In states where the bar is integrated, the courts seem to have vested a power of initiation or a power of veto in the state bar. The possibility of the exercise of this veto—possible objections raised within the bar—appears to have influenced the suggestion of the Shreveport Bar Association that approval not be sought from the Louisiana State Bar Association. There was a recognition that, if objections were raised in some quarters, the Louisiana Supreme Court would be compelled to disapprove the admission of nonresident lawyers. Similarly, the advice of the President of the State Bar of Texas about the direct approach to the Texas Supreme Court, coupled with the appearance of bar support, was to avoid a possible bar veto. Meanwhile local assent and local court accommodation works.

Our data suggest that the ways that rule changes are approached bargains into or away from the potential power of the bar to influence court action. Where the bar is hostile to change, the mere approach to the bar increases the risk that an inchoate power over admissions—or at least the desire to scrutinize admissions—will be converted to an active power. Direct application to the courts, however, does not always avoid the bar hostility. In the jurisdictions where the pilot programs have experienced the greatest difficulty, which we will examine next, frequently the bench, before it acts, will require assurance of bar support or at least evidence of nonhostility. That was the situation with the Army's pilot programs at Forts Leavenworth and Riley in Kansas and at Fort Carson in Colorado.

Kansas: [117] In Kansas the Army's efforts to implement the pilot program ran into resistance from the local bars—Geary and Riley Counties (Fort Riley) and Leavenworth County (Fort Leavenworth)—based on fear of loss of business and loss of market areas. It was also based on fear of "socialized" delivery of legal services. The local county bars expressed a view of the license to practice law which, taken at face value, would seem to indicate a concern for and control over the quality representation of clients—particularly indigent clients. Upon final analysis, however, as we shall see, the views of the county bars related more to a conception of the local license to practice law as containing a grant to a market area, like a market area which comes with a McDonald's Hamburger or

---

[117] Data on the Kansas negotiations were obtained from the files of the American Bar Association and the Army Legal Assistance Office; and from interviews with Colonel John A. Zalonis, July 9, 1971, in Washington, D.C., and Colonel Henry Olk, October 22, 1971, at Fort Riley, Kansas.

a Fuller Brush franchise. These views were parochial and were fanned by economic dependence of the local communities on the large and highly visible Army posts. Further, they were supported by state laws which talked in terms of law practice and maintenance of a law office not only within the state but within the judicial district as well.[118] Even Kansas lawyers are viewed as outsiders in Kansas when they are distant from their homes and law offices. In the end, although the status of the pilot program was in doubt, the negotiations resulted in the creation of new civilian legal aid societies where none had existed before.

The Army opened the negotiations with the civilian bars at the local-county level. Negotiations were opened informally and early, even before the Army guidelines were promulgated, because Kansas was one of the first designated sites for a pilot program. It was erroneously assumed by the Army that Kansas would be easy and New Jersey would be hard—a 180 degree misapprehension of reality. Colonel Henry Olk, who handled the negotiations for both Forts Riley and Leavenworth understood the early directives from Washington to mean that the state bar associations in states selected for pilot programs had been apprised of the nature of the program and had endorsed the experiment. Accordingly, when the approach was made at the local level both the strength of the resistance and the appeal of the resisters to the uncommitted Kansas Bar Association came as a surprise to Colonel Olk.[119] After Colonel Olk's early November 1970 meeting with the Geary County Bar Association, one of its members, a Junction City lawyer, wrote to his United States Senator, Robert Dole:

Dear Bob,
[Colonel Olk reported on a new development—the pilot program—scheduled for initiation in Kansas] By this program the JAG is to furnish legal counsel for military personnel and dependents in all civilian courts. The extent of the representation may be limited in some instances, but I understood Colonel Olk to say that lawyers from his department would, in fact, be representing military and military connected people in our civil courts in every kind of case except personal injury cases and large probate matters. By this I took him to mean that *Army lawyers would be handling everything civilian lawyers now handle* with one or two exceptions. *If.this is true, it is the first attempt that I know about where the Government is undertaking socialized law practice.* [Have you and the other members of

---

[118] KANSAS STATUTES ANNOTATED (1964) 7–104, and Supreme Court Rule 109 requiring association, in any court case, of local Kansas attorney who is resident of and *maintains* his *law office within* the *judicial district.*

[119] Interview with Colonel Olk. October 22. 1971.

the Kansas Congressional delegation been informed of this in advance of the program or in advance of the selection of Kansas as an experimental site? Have you been consulted?] [120]

Apparently the nature of the OEO legal services program had not come to the writer's attention. Or perhaps the absence of the uniform for OEO legal service lawyers had enabled the Kansas lawyer, like the Kansas farmer, to deny the policy basis upon which institutionalized delivery of legal services and subsidized wheat prices rested—i.e., society has assumed all or some of the risk.

The question of institutionalized delivery or legal services to indigent members of the society seems not to have been considered by the Leavenworth County Bar Association, either, in advance of their alert to the military program. This is evidenced by the then lack of any civilian legal aid program, and it is evidenced by the letters of a member of the Leavenworth County Bar Association. And it is evidenced by subsequent events. Upon reading for the first time about the program in the *American Bar News*, Edward Chapman wrote asking the ABA for further information, because "we intend to study this project in depth and to examine any alternatives that may be related to the project." [121] And then on January 19, 1971 he wrote to the ABA Standing Committee on Legal Assistance for Servicemen:

> *Our committee of the Leavenworth County Bar Association is strongly opposed to the pilot project as outlined to date.* It is our feeling that assistance should be given to civilians and military alike, and not to military alone, where the person is in need. We feel that there is no basis for distinction for granting legal services to needy persons. Therefore, we feel that the project should not be assigned to and run by the Department of Defense but should be something handled by the civilians for military and civilians. The type of legal services would be civilian legal services, regardless of the relationship of the needy person to a military branch.
>
> *We would like very much to have the names and addresses of persons to whom we can effectively make our views known within the American Bar Association.*
>
> I think it is significant that of all the publicity you have mentioned, none of this publicity was directed toward those communities where pilot projects were to be set up. [122]

The Chapman letter points up an issue which runs in variants throughout our study. When bar associations act, how much do they

---

[120] Letter from Howard Harper to Senator Robert Dole, November 19, 1970 (emphasis added).

[121] Letter from Edward J. Chapman, Jr., to American Bar Association, November 24, 1970.

[122] Letter from Edward J. Chapman, Jr. to Mrs. Elma Raske, Standing Committee on Legal Assistance for Servicemen, American Bar Association, January 19, 1971 (emphasis added).

take into account the feelings of those against whose interests, or for whose interests, they claim to act? The issue cuts both ways. At times, to avoid parochial discussion within the bar, the boards of bar associations have not put the question of approval of the pilot programs to the general membership. At times, as if to bargain for the display of parochialism, the question has been put to the general membership—as was the case in San Diego, California. There remain beyond this, however, the persistent questions: When the interest of the clients or the public may be in conflict with the interests of some of the members of a bar who should the association speak for?[123] Who do they speak for?

After the evidenced hostility of the local bars, Colonel Olk shifted to a search for approval at the state level. He rejected a legislative approach after there was some indication that the legislature felt that it was a matter for the state Supreme Court. Previously, however, a Justice on that Court—a reserve officer in the Army JAG Corps—had pointed out difficulties with the existing Kansas rules and had suggested that an approach be made to the Military Law Section of the Kansas Bar Association.[124] This was tantamount to inviting bar clearance before approaching the Court. The rules the Justice alluded to were the statute and the Court rule requiring the appearance of a local Kansas attorney who has his office in the judicial district.[125] Kansas court rules allow *pro hac vice* admissions, but only if Section 7–104 of the state statutes is followed, only if there is a local attorney of record. Thoughts of asking for a rule change from the Court without going to the state Bar Association were rejected; Colonel Olk, in addition to Army guidelines about seeking bar cooperation, had some doubts about his standing to petition the court without bar concurrence.[126]

The Kansas Bar Association was first approached through the Military Law Section, whch was hospitable to the pilot program, but also was beginning to feel intramural pressures. The Chairman of the Section, Harold Chase, former Lieutenant-Governor of Kansas, sent a memorandum to the president of the state bar, the presidents of local bars throughout the state that might be affected by the pilot program, the Chairman of the Kansas House Judiciary Committee, and the Chief Justice of the Kansas Supreme Court suggest-

---

[123] *See* F. MARKS, with K. LESWING and B. FORTINSKY, THE LAWYER, THE PUBLIC, AND PROFESSIONAL RESPONSIBILITY (1972).

[124] Letter from Justice Earl E. O'Connor to Colonel Zalonis, November 23, 1970.

[125] *See* note 118 *supra*.

[126] Interview with Colonel Olk, October 22, 1971.

ing cooperation and some changes in the rules which would allow military lawyers "to defend" military personnel in civilian courts. The Section Chairman recognized that the restriction "to defend" was "half a loaf" and purposely suggested it as a compromise. He noted, in passing:

> To simply reply to the [military] request for assistance by saying "You can't do it in Kansas" without suggestion for providing legal service to a class who may be not only in need but are certainly deserving, would be unworthy of a lawyer's responsibility to the profession. Further, it must be remembered that military officer-lawyers . . . are "brothers at the bar." [127]

The military clients are seen as "deserving poor" and the military lawyer as deserving professionals.

On February 1, 1971 the president of the Kansas Bar Association asked one officer of the association and one member of the Executive Council to be an *ad hoc* committee to look into the question and make recommendations to the Executive Council. The member of the Executive Council was Howard Harper, of Junction City, who had certainly been a steady, open, and avowed opponent of the pilot program from the time he wrote the "socialism" letter to Senator Dole and most likely before. The issues put to the two-man committee by the president were:

1. What will be the impact on our judicial and professional system of allowing a group of miiltary lawyers not permanently situated or regularly practicing in Kansas to render professional services and appear in court without examination or other qualification for admission and especially without being subject to the control that courts historically exercise over members of the Bar who continuously practice before them and must maintain their standing in the local community by integrity and good professional work?
2. Will the members of the military service who depend on this group for advice and representation be better represented than they now are?
3. Is our system of requiring people with legal problems to be represented by independent practicing attorneys really threatened professionally or economically by this proposal for what really amounts to organized group legal aid; shortly put, is this a step toward government control or socialization of the profession?
4. Is there really a need for legal aid for members of the military service stationed in this state and if there is, is there a better way to deal with it than the one proposed? [128]

---

[127] Chairman, Military Law Section, Kansas Bar Association, Memorandum re: Proposal by Department of Defense for Expanded Program of Legal Assistance to Military Personnel (January 11, 1971).

[128] Letter from Robert Martin to Marvin E. Thompson and Howard W. Harper, February 1, 1971.

The result: "Support" of the pilot program by the Kansas Bar Association, severely limited and subject to a power to veto vested in the local county bar associations; still no pilot program in Kansas; but one definite and one aborning legal aid society.

On June 18, 1971 the Executive Council of the Kansas Bar Association passed a resolution which announced support for the expanded military legal assistance program through the establishment of a "properly supported pilot or test program . . . subject to the limitations hereinafter set out." [129] The form of the abstract endorsement was faintly reminiscent of the ABA endorsement. And the limitations made it clear that the Kansas Bar, like the ABA, was going to let the decisions be made locally. The important limitations were:

2. (a) Only available to enlisted grade of E–4 and below, "who file an affidavit to the effect that they have no funds or resources from which to pay civilian counsel." [130]

    (b) "The legal assistance officers assigned to the project shall consist only of those military personnel who have been admitted to practice by the Supreme Court of Kansas . . . under Rules of the Supreme Court . . . as may be amended which comprise the following: [Reciprocity admission, examination, temporary admission, and association with attorney who is a member of the Kansas bar.]" [131]

    (d) The client shall be advised of the right to civilian counsel at his own expense, and shall sign a statement indicating his choice of the military or civilian counsel. [132]

    (e) If client chooses civilian counsel, the legal officer shall show client a telephone listing or legal directory of lawyers within or in the counties adjoining the military establishment. [133]

    (j) *"Prior to accepting a client under the program, the . . . legal assistance officer shall refer the matter to civilian legal service agencies, such as a legal aid society, lawyer referral or other similar type group, agency, organization or committee established by the bar association located in a county contiguous to the military establishment to which the client is assigned by military order."* [134]

"3.   This resolution shall not be or become effective as to military personnel stationed, or assigned to duty, at Fort Riley,

---

[129] Executive Council, Kansas Bar Association, Resolution for the Implementation of an Expanded Program of Legal Assistance to Military Personnel Within the State of Kansas (June 18, 1971), sec. 1.

[130] *Id.*, sec. 2(a).

[131] *Id.*, sec. 2(b).

[132] *Id.*, sec. 2(d).

[133] *Id.*, sec. 2(e).

[134] *Id.*, sec. 2(j).

Kansas until its contents have been approved by a *majority vote of the combined membership* of the *Geary* and *Riley County*, Kansas, Bar Associations who are currently engaged in the active practice of law in their respective counties. [Similar provision for Fort Leavenworth and Leavenworth County Bar Association]." [135]

The Riley County Bar was already on record as rejecting the plan, because (1) military lawyers are unfamiliar with Kansas law and Kansas courts, (2) the court appointment system for felonies works for servicemen, (3) eligibility criteria are vague, and (4) after approval the scope of service would expand.[136] They continued to be opposed through October 1971 when the field work for this study was finished.

The Leavenworth County Bar Association has not as explicitly opposed the pilot program nor have they supported it. But their position has been more than silence. When the program at Fort Leavenworth considered going ahead with its Kansas-admitted judge advocate as the lawyer in charge of the office and the other lawyers "associated with him," the staff judge advocate there was told informally by some of the members of the local bar that the Kansas lawyer would not be eligible under Kansas rules, because he did not have this office within the judicial district—it being on federal territory.[137] Furthermore, the Leavenworth County Bar Association took an action which had the effect under the state bar Resolution of blocking the program; they formed a section (j) legal aid society. As a gesture they have invited military lawyers from the fort to join with them on the board of the legal aid society.

The Geary County Bar Association has taken no action subsequent to the state bar resolution, but they, too, are considering a section (j) legal aid society.

In sum: The Army feels stymied in Kansas. "No" is the message. But nobody wants to say it plainly. There has been an abundance of committee consideration but no definitive action. The legislature is unlikely to act without Court acquiescence and Kansas Bar Association approval. And, meaningful state bar approval has already been blunted by the adoption of the local option formula.[138]

---

[135] *Id.*, sec. 3.

[136] Letter from President of Riley County Bar Association to Chief Justice of Kansas Supreme Court, May 3, 1971.

[137] Report of Staff Judge Advocate at Fort Leavenworth, Lt. Col. Robert Boyer, February 1, 1971.

[138] The Kansas experience should be contrasted with the Army's experience at Fort Huachuca, Arizona, where the local bar approved the admission of nonresident military officers for purposes of the pilot program, got the State Bar of

Colorado: [139] In Colorado, as in Kansas, the opposition came from a local bar—the El Paso County Association where the Army's pilot program site, Fort Carson, is located. The Denver Bar Association and the Colorado Bar Association have endorsed the pilot program. And the Colorado Supreme Court seems to be open to the need for a program, but there has been hesitancy on the part of both the Court and the state bar association to face the El Paso bar with a *fait accompli.* At this writing a committee of the Supreme Court is attempting to work out a resolution of the problem satisfactory to all parties.

Although the Army's pilot program at Fort Carson was the basic program being sought, the Navy, too, sought a pilot operation in Colorado which would use Colorado reservists exclusively—Naval Reserve Law Company 9–3 of Denver, Colorado. Active duty, retirement, and other credits would be earned. The Commanding Officer of that Company, John Law, handled both the Navy and Army negotiations for rule changes that would be required for special licensing of nonresident lawyers. The Army wanted a Colorado lawyer to act as negotiator. On closer examination, however, only the Army's negotiations were important because Colorado lawyers agreeing to represent an indigent population or cooperating with a military legal assistance program toward that end would need no special approval. As a matter of fact, the Colorado Bar Association on April 24, 1971 did easily approve the Navy Law Company pilot program:

> The Board of Governors of the Colorado Bar Association approves the performance of legal services and assistance *by members of the Bar of the State of Colorado* who are performing such services as inactive duty members of reserve components of the Armed Services under the Department of Defense Legal Assistance Pilot Program for military personnel and their dependents, who are unable to pay the fee for a civilian lawyer, on the condition that such services may be provided only on the same basis and standards of eligibility as those presently extended by the Office of Economic Opportunity.[140]

Perhaps because of the dual negotiations, the approach was made first to the Denver and Colorado Bar Associations. The Board of Trustees of the Denver Bar unanimously approved the use of out-of-state lawyers in the military pilot program. And the Lawyers Re-

Arizona to go along, and the State Bar is now petitioning the Arizona Supreme Court for those special admissions.

[139] The data from Colorado were obtained from reports and documents in both the Navy and Army files in Washington.

[140] Resolution of Colorado Bar Association, April 24, 1971.

ferral Service Committee of the Colorado Bar Association approved a resolution which included:

> That the Board of Governors recommend to the Supreme Court of the State of Colorado the adoption of a rule of court permitting special admission to the Bar of this State of active duty Judge Advocates who have been admitted to the Bar of another state . . . for the special purpose of performing legal assistance to military personnel and their dependents . . . on the same basis as such services are being performed by [OEO].[141]

Meanwhile, however, the El Paso County Bar Association was taking a hard position: Absolutely not! The El Paso opposition was not explicitly framed in terms of loss of business but rather in general terms that do not foreclose that view. The phrases "government encroachment" and "the government wants to get the camel's nose under the tent" were heard. Creeping socialism, in other words.

The opposition of the El Paso County Bar Association was communicated to the Board of Governors of the Colorado Bar Association, which in the face of the local opposition was disinclined to act. (This was at the same meeting that endorsed the Navy Law Company plan.) Similarly, the two-justice committee of the Supreme Court, which has the power to recommend rule changes, was initially disinclined to act unless the Colorado Bar Association were to indicate a disposition to move ahead on a rule change—this, even though Colorado is not an integrated bar state. The Supreme Court committee is, however, actively seeking to bring the parties together on the issue of a hospitable rule change.

California: [142] Local opposition was only part of the story with the Navy's program in San Diego, California. The character of the local opposition, however, coupled with what seemed to be general opposition in the state to any admission of nonresident lawyers, led the Navy to revise the goals for its San Diego program. The local opposition was not so uniform or so intense as in Kansas and Colorado. There was, however, some attempt to make it so. In the end there was a stand-off "approval" of a modified program. The program is now operating in San Diego without a written agreement; California lawyers make all court appearances.

Letters advising of the pilot program were originally sent to the

---

[141] Draft Resolution of Colorado Bar Association, proposed by Lawyer Referral Service Committee, January 15, 1971.

[142] Data regarding this negotiation were obtained from reports and memoranda in the Navy Legal Assistance Office, Washington, D.C., and from interviews with Charles Froelich, former President of the San Diego Bar Association, August 11, 1971, and Lt. Commander Ervin Riddle, August 12, 1971.

Presidents of the San Diego County Bar Association and the State Bar of California. Statements of position and comments on program were invited.[143] The president of the San Diego Bar Association referred the matter to the Military Liaison Committee. The Navy was informed of the need for study "because of the important implications for the local bar." [144] The Military Liaison Committee reported back to the President, closely divided on the issue, but technically in favor of endorsing the experiment. The Committee had divided into subcommittees which considered three "problem" areas: (1) qualifications of military lawyers to participate in the pilot program; (2) eligibility for services under the program; and (3) the scope of services offered. The report of the committee summarized these subcommittee findings and also included a discussion of "general policy considerations." [145] On the issue of qualifications, the committee concluded that lawyers appearing in court or on pleadings must be members of the California bar; that this requirement was statutory—being the enactment of the integrated bar rule.[146] Any change, according to the committee, had to come through the legislature; one member of the committee felt that the California Supreme Court had inherent power to change the rules or grant special licenses. The committee suggested the use of California reservists to augment the California lawyers who might be on active duty, "with local Judge Advocates associating with the attorney for the purposes of assisting in the preparation of cases." [147] After reaching its conclusions about California lawyers only, the committee curiously suggests that the whole issue be passed to the state bar association.

On the issue of eligibility, even though the Navy guidelines called for service to E–3 and below, the committee wanted the criteria more strictly drawn and more explicitly tied into OEO poverty standards. The chairman reported:

> Certain members . . . were of the opinion that regardless of the guidelines adopted, the ultimate effect would be the elimination of some paying business.[148]

---

[143] Letters from Commandant, 11th Naval District to Charles W. Froelich, Jr., and Forrest A. Plant, January 18, 1971.

[144] Letter from Froelich to Commandant, January 29, 1971.

[145] Report from John R. Wingert, Chairman of Military Liaison Committee, to Froelich, February 4, 1971.

[146] CALIFORNIA BUSINESS AND PROFESSIONS CODE, secs. 6000 *et seq.*, specifically 6125.

[147] Report, *supra* note 145 at 4.

[148] *Id.*, at 6.

This opinion was an amalgam of those who felt they were presently deriving fees from those below the E-3 grade[149] and those who believed that the eligibility criteria would rise once the institutionalized delivery were accepted.

The committee's major comment on scope was the elimination of criminal matters because of the availability of the public defender. (The San Diego program did drop criminal defense in view of this recommendation and in view of the excellence of the public defender program in the area.) The committee also felt that because of available manpower in the 11th Naval District—military lawyers—the amount of service offered should be reduced.

Under the "General Policy Considerations" the committee report again raised the issue of an inadequate staff of lawyers to handle the array of matters contemplated by the pilot program. This time, however, the point was aimed more directly at the quality of representation. An additional point was made:

> It is generally believed that the junior Navy lawyer does not possess the practical experience required to successfully handle the civil matters contemplated. Few, if any, Navy lawyers, whether senior or junior in rank, stationed in the Eleventh Naval District have had any actual experience in the civilian practice of law. Consequently, junior Navy lawyers would not be able to obtain any experienced guidance from their superiors. Likewise, Navy law clerks and associated civil service employees are probably unqualified by reason of lack of experience, to handle the clerical end of this program.[150]

The sincerity of this concern will have to be judged from the context. How serious is the concern may depend on how these same professional responsibilities are handled vis-a-vis the already admitted California lawyer. The following parts of the report came before and after the concern about quality and experience:

> One opinion held by a number of members of the Committee is that this program is simply another form of socialized legal services and will eliminate a valuable source of income from the private practitioner.
> One opinion expressed by some members of the Committee was that the expanded legal assistance program, like other government supported legal offices rendering services to the poor, would concern itself more with class actions rather than representing the individual needs of the clients. It was also suggested that the percentage of civil cases appealed would increase because of this program, since no fee would

---

[149] One lawyer wrote, in part, "Over 50% of my practice and probably that of most lawyers in the area is with Navy families. I can assure you that many of my clients are in the pay grades contemplated to be covered by this program."

[150] Report, *supra* note 145.

be charged to the serviceman or his dependent for the attorney's work in this regard.[151]

These statements reflect feelings about the client, the earnings of fellow lawyers—dilution of craft or market—and feelings about OEO legal services (opposed bitterly in San Diego) and concern about the increase of the appellate docket, all rolled into one. While the report of the Military Liaison Committee was being awaited, the president of the State Bar of California had referred the Navy request to the Board of Governors. He later reported the action of the Board, informing the Navy of the restrictions in the Business and Professions Code against nonadmitted lawyers appearing in California, and stated:

> Because of conflict with laws of State, the State Bar is unable to enter into any agreement which would recognize the propriety of the practice of law in this State by persons who are not members of the California Bar.
> . . .
>
> In addition to the problem of probable unauthorized practice of law, it has been observed that other problems, analogous to those which have arisen during the inception of other programs providing legal services for the poor, may also arise in connection with the pilot programs. These problems too should be considered in any such discussions.[152]

Again, comes the reference to the California Rural Legal Assistance Program, and other OEO programs in California—a concern centering around "law reform" issues. By informal communication, the Navy tried to distinguish their program from the "law reform" programs by pointing to the basic reasons for the enlargement of the legal assistance program in the first place—the felt need to serve the legal needs of their troops. This would be consistent with an individual service model of a legal service program and not a law reform model.[153] The McCartin Report, too, was ample authority—the military felt as threatened by class actions and affirmative litigation as did the California and San Diego base. (In fact, the program excluded a law reform approach.) The Navy went further, however, in the informal negotiations, and suggested that Navy officer-lawyers were not as phrenetic as their colleagues in OEO and besides they were more subject to discipline. Hair style comparisons were made in these reassuring remarks. This argument may have been satisfactory and comforting to the San Diego bar, but the possibilities of such control and the flattening of the law reform urge was a negative, as we shall see, for the Alaska bar.

---

[151] *Id.*, at 8.

[152] Letter from Plant to Commandant, 11th Naval District, February 23, 1971.

[153] *See* F. R. MARKS, THE LEGAL NEEDS OF THE POOR: A CRITICAL ANALYSIS (American Bar Foundation Legal Services for the Poor Series, 1971).

When the San Diego Bar Association Board of Governors met on February 8, 1971 to consider the report of the Military Liaison Committee, they rejected even the possibility of endorsing the pilot program in principle, concluding that the bar "was not in favor of implementation of the proposed program." [154] The reasons assigned were primarily opposition to non-California lawyers appearing in California courts. However, the thread of concern about the military services spreading themselves too thin remained, as did concern about legal service programs generally.[155] The Navy appealed from this position by asking for an opportunity for its Judge Advocate General—Rear Admiral Joseph B. McDevitt—to address the general membership of the San Diego Bar Association; to explain the Navy's program, and to "reassure" them of the nonthreatening nature of the program.

Admiral McDevitt addressed a luncheon meeting of the San Diego County Bar Association on March 19, 1971, attended by between 250 and 300 lawyers, which is a huge turnout for that Association. The story behind the turnout is illuminating. The announcement of the meeting, in leaflet-handbill style, was sent to all lawyers in the area.[156] On the top was a cartoon depicting a small ship with a crew labeled "Navy lawyers" on one side of an island—apparently the old legal assistance program—and a large battleship on the other side of the island. The battleship was named "U.S.S. Navy Lawship." On the island was a depiction of the San Diego County Courthouse. In bold type at the top of the announcement (under the Bar letterhead):

> NAVY LAWYERS IN CIVILIAN COURTS?
> Excursion or Invasion?
> It Depends On Your Point Of View.

There followed:

> So come listen to Rear Adm. Joseph B. McDevitt . . .
> If your practice includes family, probate, criminal,
> personal injury or bankruptcy, this program is of
> *great interest* to you.
>   DON'T MISS THIS JOINT MEETING . . .
>
> This Room seats only 350. Meeting is first come,
> first serve. Don't wait for radio, television and

---

[154] Letter from Froelich to Commandant 11th Naval District, February 11, 1971.

[155] *Id.*

[156] Announcement of March 19, 1971, monthly meeting of the San Diego County Bar Association.

newspaper coverage. Find out for yourself what's
going on.

Come, let us reason together! The large turnout is hardly surprising. Neither is the refusal of the San Diego bar to change its position after the post-meeting reconsideration. This time, however, the reasons assigned for refusal sounded more concern about the caliber of law practice by military lawyers: military lawyers would be unfamiliar with California laws and with how things were done in the local courts. This time the Board of the San Diego County Bar Association also suggested that the funds for such a program be used to augment OEO services.

A stalemate developed, until the Navy felt that it needed to proceed with the San Diego pilot program. A written agreement embodying a modified plan was proffered to the San Diego County Bar Association.[157] It contained 15 points, including assurances of no threat to sources of income to the civilian bar, agreement to offer cases to the public defender and legal aid before taking cases, and, most important:

> All appearances in California courts will be made by a military lawyer who is an active member of California State Bar in compliance with the Business and Professions Code.[158]

In response, the President of the San Diego County Bar Association wrote:

> As a personal matter I find nothing objectionable about any of the 15 points contained in your letter. Having consulted with the Executive Committee of our Board of Directors, however, I am impressed with the fact that this is a matter of *some delicacy*. There is reluctance by certain of our members to enter into any "agreement" even though the precise terms of same may be quite acceptable. . . . It will be necessary to bring the matter before the Board on June 14, 1971.[159]

On June 23, 1971 the President of the San Diego County Bar Association ended the "negotiations" with a report of the Board Action, which was to decline execution of any agreement. The president indicated that the formal action was not a disapproval of any of the various items—most of which were "appropriate." He said:

> [We have] little or no jurisdiction. . . . The program as presented is not subject to the Bar's criticism; neither is it, in the Bar's opinion, appropriate for its approval or ratification.
>
> The details and mechanisms of your program remain to be implemented

---

[157] Letter from Commandant, 11th Naval District, to Froelich, May 20, 1971.
[158] *Id.*
[159] Letter from Froelich to Commandant, 11th Naval District, June 2, 1971.

by military lawyers who are licensed to practice in California. While the Bar is reluctant to take a position as an organization in support of this overall program, it nevertheless remains the Bar's responsibility to assist all California lawyers, including military lawyers, in the performance of their professional responsibilities. If, therefore, the Bar or any of its committees, including our Military Liaison Committee, can be of any aid in specific problems or procedures, please feel free to call upon us.[160]

This was neither a victory nor a defeat for the Navy. It was unable to use out-of-state lawyers in its program. The Navy did have to compromise, and it ended up with the program it could have had without approaching the bar. But tacit blessings were bestowed by the local bar—in the last paragraph of the bar president's letter. The Navy program is now in operation at San Diego along the lines of the proffered 15-point agreement.

The bars of Riley, Geary, and Leavenworth Counties, Kansas, and El Paso County, Colorado, rejected the pilot program without serious attention paid to what was or was not in the clients' interests. The clients were not considered as central. Not so in the case of the San Diego County Bar Association. Clients may not have been central to the deliberations, but issues of quality representation, experience, and competence were at least raised, as was the issue of who could better serve the clients. The charge of inexperience merits closer examination. The committee had suggested that Navy lawyers would be inexperienced in the type of matters being handled. The assertion has merit. But, again, the double standard; the context of the assertion raises questions about its weight. All lawyers, whether they be admitted to the California bar or elsewhere, at the beginning, and continuing for new matters, are inexperienced. Law practice consists of representing clients in the handling of their problems. New clients, new demands, new situations, and new laws are continually placing the lawyer in the position of being inexperienced. From the clients' viewpoint, and from the higher interests of the profession, the issues are more properly: Under what circumstances will a lawyer become experienced? What will be his supervision during the period of acquiring the experience? What training will he receive after he receives his license? For that point is the beginning, not the end, of a lawyer's acquisition of skill. To substitute the magic of a bar examination and the magic of a local law license for these harder questions is to mask the true meaning of inexperience and incompetence. For a profession that still lets its general practitioners do the equivalent of delicate brain surgery,

---

[160] Letter from Froelich to Commandant, 11th Naval District, June 23, 1971.

it ill behooves a local guild to say: Our perhaps inexperienced lawyers are better than your perhaps inexperienced lawyers. Though from guild identification the first "perhaps" would usually read "most assuredly." The point is well exemplified by the San Diego lawyer who interposed the probable unfamiliarity of nonresident lawyers with the California no fault divorce law; a law which postdates the admission of about 97 percent of the lawyers admitted to practice in California. There is irony to the suggestion, when one considers that the no-fault law simplified procedures for divorce, even to the point of stimulating *pro se* appearances.

The problems of relative inexperience are questions of training, supervision, and exposure—familiarity with either the array of problems of particular clients or the specific problems of an array of clients. For initial training—law school—the Judge Advocates General say they screen applicants, accepting lawyers from the top quarter of their class. They insist on training in courts martial and other problems of military justice, a training they formally apply. And, in connection with the pilot program, the military services have taken the view that the judge advocates must be trained and supervised in connection with the matters they will be handling. Short of a law office practice, is there a similar mechanism—a similar requirement—for locally admitted lawyers? Even California, with one of the better continuing education programs, has no way of supervising the application of the post-admission training. It is optional for the individual attorney. In some instances, as at Forts Monmouth and Dix, the local OEO lawyers are assisting in the training, augmented by local members of the bar. The Legal Aid Society is doing the training in Hawaii, too. In other instances, as in Florida, reserve judge advocates will conduct the training sessions and help develop the training materials. To the extent the military program fails to adequately supervise or train the pilot program lawyers in local law and practice, the legitimate fears of the local bar are indeed justified.

The remaining element is: Who is in the best position to communicate with and understand the military client and his problems, the military lawyer or the civilian lawyer? Surely, this is important. And it is by no means simple. There is the question of command influence, which was raised seriously in the Alaska negotiations. There also is the question of how the military client feels about his lawyer when he is also a superior officer. Such questions are important, but they are not answered by facile reference to license. In sum: The issues of competence, experience, preparation, and training are separate from the issue of license. The blurring of the lines between the issues during negotiations, such as those conducted in California, raise questions about whether the discussants have substituted rhetoric for reason and whether they have, even for themselves and their own—members of the local bar—defined what a lawyer is and what his role should be.

Alaska: [161] The Alaska Bar Association opposed the joint Air Force-Army pilot program at Elmendorf Air Force Base and Fort Richardson, Anchorage, Alaska. The opposition seemed atypical. It was based, for the most part, on distrust of the military and fear of an intrusion by the military into the lawyer-client relationship. There was a feeling that the privileged nature of client communications and the integrity of the lawyer-client relationship would be compromised by command influence and by the record keeping requirements of the pilot program. Market intrusion did not appear to play a major role, as it had in other jurisdictions. But long-run views about protecting the Alaska Bar from too easy admission by "outsiders" probably played some part in the rejection of the program. Alaska, an integrated bar state, offered a striking example of the abdication of judicial authority over the issue of admission.

There was precedent for special admission to the Alaska courts, although there was no formally recognized procedure. It was bar and not court supervised. For years a lawyer on the staff of a federal or state agency, who had been admitted to the bars of other states, had been granted waiver of strict admission standards by the Board of Governors of the Alaska Bar Association so that he could practice until the next bar examination. This waiver was similarly accorded to OEO and VISTA lawyers. The military relied on this practice in Alaska when developing the site selections for the pilot program. There was no reason to assume that the full-scale program, with admission of all judge advocates, could not be launched in Alaska. What was not understood was the recent sharp and rapid departure from this relaxed standard in Alaska. The discovery of oil on the North Slope and the resulting surge of enterprise was reflected in the increase in the number of lawyers. Five years ago approximately 150 lawyers held licenses in Alaska. Today there are over 500. Easy admission has been replaced by rigid requirements, including the

---

[161] The data on the Alaska negotiations were gathered from reports and correspondence in Washington, D.C., and from interviews with Colonels Arnold C. Castle and Robert Frasier, USAF; Col. John Webb and Lt. Col. George Harrison, U.S.A.; Peter LaBate, President, Mary La Follette, Executive Director, and Ralph Crews, Chairman of the Military Legal Assistance Program Committee, Alaska Bar Association; and Chief Justice George F. Boney and Associate Justice John H. Dimond, the Supreme Court of Alaska.

giving—by contract—of the California Bar Examination. And there was open hostility to further waivers. This change affected, in advance, the way that the Alaska Bar dealt with the military program. A collateral change also had an effect on the character of the objections raised. Because of the rapid growth of the bar and the frontier quality of life in Alaska, the new arrivals had brought the average age of Alaska lawyer to *below 30*. It followed that the bar had a somewhat liberal outlook. An antipathy to the military was encountered. But it was a different hostility than had been encountered from the organized bar elsewhere. It was a hostility based on distrust, a distrust tutored by the war in Southeast Asia and the draft.

The Air Force presumably was in charge of negotiations for the program. Its approach was directly to the President of the Alaska Bar Association, by letter, outlining the pilot program and asking for advice. Meanwhile, the Army, following its own guidelines, but not coordinating efforts with the Air Force, was seeking "the cooperation of local bars." Before the Alaska Bar Association had had an opportunity to meet and consider the Air Force request, the Army had appeared before the Anchorage Bar Association and the Federal Bar Association, at Anchorage, and the Fairbanks Bar Association. The Fairbanks area, at the time, was depressed because of "temporary" stoppage of the Alaska pipe line. The town was experiencing a 25 percent unemployment rate. While the lawyers in Anchorage did not appear threatened by possible encroachments on fee-generating business, their colleagues in Fairbanks did. (The Air Force planned a second pilot program at Eilson Air Force Base at Fairbanks.) The Fairbanks bar was shown the McCartin Report and seized upon the Martin (Coast Guard) Comments to document their concern that the military program would not be kept to the poverty level airmen. But, more important, and perhaps to better argue their cause, the Fairbanks bar seized upon another issue and gave it wide currency: The record keeping and command supervision over the program would compromise the integrity of the lawyer-client relationship. An unfortunate draft release form contributed to the making of this issue. The release form, to be signed by clients, allowed reports of the matter to be sent to Washington. The form seemed to go beyond the statistical needs of the experimental pilot program, which are really the same as any other legal service program. The overbreadth of the form was unintentional, but the damage had been done; a major issue was framed.

The Fairbanks bar sent letters to the Alaska Bar Association featuring this issue. In addition, several Fairbanks lawyers attended the Federal and Anchorage bar association meetings, raising the issue of command influence, and citing the release form. The Anchorage Bar Association passed a resolution against the pilot program. The following reasons for that action have been cited:

(1) There would be no control by the Alaska Bar over the military lawyer's representation of clients.
(2) There would be no confidentiality of client records. The lawyer-client privilege would be breached.
(3) There was suspicion of the military with respect to its concern over the rights of individual clients; there would be other (intermediary) influences affecting the defense of criminal causes, for example.
(4) The pay of military people should be raised.[162]

The first reason cited has to do with both admissions and discipline questions; the quality of the lawyers in the first place and their amenability to discipline. Disciplinary jurisdiction problems have been raised in many states. Uncertainty has rested on a paucity of literature and case material. Nobody has suggested, however, that an admitting court, even one admitting a lawyer *pro hac vice*, lacks authority over the lawyer admitted. The power to supervise and discipline is inherent, even though the practice is not prevalent. The admission can be withdrawn. Further, nobody has suggested that a court admitting a nonresident lawyer is in a worse position than a client in the state of a lawyer's admission to raise, by complaint, issues of professional misconduct or breach of professional standards. The issue is not standing. It is comity. The concern over disciplinary powers like the concern over quality of representation may embody a double standard. Is there a bar association or a disciplinary agency that has been so outstanding in its exercise of self-regulation of the local bar that it can concern itself with the issue of "perfecting jurisdiction" over the standards of outside lawyers? I have yet to find one. Rather, one discerns a reprise of the experience and quality refrains: ours we can and do *not* regulate, yours we have questions about.

The Alaska Bar Association took no action on the Air Force-Army request at its January 24, 1971 quarterly meeting at Juneau. There was a discussion, however, and during its course the Air Force agreed to have judge advocates take a special examination on Alaska law as a way of assuring the bar and bench that adequate training about local rules and practices will have occurred. The President of the Alaska Bar, Millard Ingram, appointed a special committee to

---

[162] These reasons were advanced by Peter LaBate in an interview on September 27, 1971.

study the expanded program. The special committee, chaired by an Air Force reserve officer, had five members: the public defender, a representative from Alaska Legal Services Corporation (the OEO program), a Fairbanks lawyer, and an Anchorage lawyer. The committee chairman reported to the President of the Alaska Bar Association:

> The majority of the committee feels that although such a program has been shown to be necessary, that it should be handled by organizations already in existence and performing that type of work, such as the Alaska Legal Services, Public Defender, etc.[163]

This position was urged by the public defender and the OEO program representative on the committee. The report went on to deal with the concern about command influence:

> [If the program is implemented], the majority feels that military lawyers representing indigents should physically office in the facilities housing the agencies already in this type of work, such as OEO, Public Defender, etc. The general feeling underlying this recommendation was, that there would be more integrity in the attorney-client relationship as opposed to command influence that might be exercised over lawyers handling the program were they officing on a military reservation. My *personal* feeling is that there is no danger of command influence in such an area as this, because of my past experience as a JAG officer and long-time observations of JAG activities as a Reserve Officer. However, the majority of the committee felt this way. I further feel, *personally*, that such a suggestion would be impractical because of the inconvenience of these offices to military personnel who mostly live on base. There is also some feeling that there might be some antagonism between attorneys working for OEO, Public Defender, etc., and a career military officer.[164]

The committee, with its chairman dissenting, went on to recommend that no civil matters be handled, and that the program use Alaska lawyers, only; recommending that *no* waivers be granted on account of the military program.

The Board of Governors of the Alaska Bar Association adopted the report of the committee at its May 24, 1971 meeting. The following is an excerpt from the minutes of that meeting:

> Following agreement by the Board that approval of the majority report meant, as a practical matter, that a program would not be implemented without further action from the Board of Governors [the report was adopted].[165]

---

[163] Letter from Ralph Crews to Millard Ingram, May 4, 1971.

[164] *Id.*, at 2.

[165] Minutes, Meeting of Board of Governors, Alaska Bar Association, May 24, 1971.

And they were right. Although the Air Force subsequently made a direct request to the Alaska Supreme Court for a special rule, no action has been taken, because in Alaska no action can be taken without the assent of the organized bar. The Air Force request was referred by the Court to the Alaska bar for formal recommendations. Further, the Court, which appeared disposed toward implementing the program, invited the parties to a conference in October.[166] Nothing came of this conference. Nothing will unless the bar recedes from its position. The Alaska Supreme Court is willing to mediate but unwilling to enter an order in the face of bar opposition.[167] There is a history to this position. As a result of an open and acrimonious fight between the Supreme Court of Alaska and the Alaska bar over who had the ultimate right to initiate and terminate disciplinary proceedings and who had the right to amend the rules of admission and discipline—a fight which saw the assets of the Alaska Bar Association impounded by the Court—a compact between the bench and the bar was entered into. It provided that there would be no change in rules pertaining to admission and discipline *unless initiated* by the bar association and approved by the Court. While many, including some of the justices, believe this compact is an invalid delegation of judicial authority, nobody feels that the test of the compact will come over the military legal assistance program.

Hawaii: [168] In Hawaii, the Navy's experience was the reverse of the Air Force experience in Alaska: A written agreement, providing for a Massachusetts-type order, was agreed to by the Navy, the Bar Association of Hawaii, and the Legal Aid Society of Hawaii, but the Supreme Court of Hawaii refused to either enter into any agreement or entertain the entry of an order which would facilitate court appearances by nonresident legal assistance officers. The negotiations with the bar ran smoothly. The Legal Aid Society supported and forwarded the Navy's position in the negotiations—another contrast to Alaska.

The agreement between the Navy, the Bar Association, and the Legal Aid Society eliminated criminal cases. It was felt that the

---

[166] Letter from Chief Justice George F. Boney to Colonel Arnold Castle, September 15, 1971.

[167] Interview with Chief Justice George F. Boney, September 27, 1971.

[168] The data for the negotiations in Hawaii were gathered from reports and letters in the Legal Assistance Office, U.S. Navy, Washington, D.C., and from interviews with Commander Herbert Woolley, at Pearl Harbor; Leslie Lum, President of the Bar Association of Hawaii; J. M. Rolls, Chairman of Bar Association Committee on Pilot Program; and, Ronald Y. C. Yee, General Counsel, Legal Aid Society of Hawaii, all of Honolulu.

Public Defender covered this area well. As already indicated, it originally provided for a Massachusetts-type order. And it provided for joint supervision of the eligibility standards, which were pegged to "the standards from time to time utilized by the Legal Aid Society." The agreement provides that the screening interview will be conducted by a judge advocate, who shall, in the first instance, apply the eligibility standards. He will then send the information to the Legal Aid Society for their concurrence on eligibility. There is a provision for Bar Association review if the Navy and Legal Aid do not concur. In actual practice, the screenings provisions have been operated with less formality, by telephone conversations and mutual trust.

At an early bar meeting on the Navy plan, Chief Justice Richardson of the Supreme Court of Hawaii was present and indicated a disinclination to amend or alter Supreme Court Rule 15 (the admissions rule),[169] even though the bar might favor such a rule. Unlike Alaska, the Hawaii Court is jealous of its prerogatives. Previously the Court had rejected an integrated bar rule suggested by the bar. Too, it had rejected a rule that would have enabled nonlawyers, clerks, to attend calendar calls for lawyers. The Chief Justice was of the opinion that either Navy lawyers should take the bar examination in Hawaii or the Navy should proceed with Hawaiian lawyers only. That is what the Navy has done, commenced the pilot program with Navy lawyers who were locally admitted. Further, the Navy and the Bar submitted to the Court a formal petition for the Amendment of Rule 15. That petition is currently pending.

Florida: [170] The Florida Supreme Court, like the Alaska Supreme Court, felt that bar initiative and approval were essential to any amendment of the integrated bar rule or any order facilitating the administration of the pilot program. Unlike the Air Force negotiation in Alaska, however, there were special factors which contributed to the fact that a pilot program is now operating at Pensacola Naval Air Station. The Navy negotiator, Commander Robert Newton, was sensitive to the felt needs of the bar and sought to accommodate his requests for bar approval to those needs. The initial draft of the proposed written agreement sought the appearance of out-of-state lawyers in Florida courts, but only when Florida lawyers appeared

---

[169] 43 Reports, Supreme Court Rule 15b.

[170] The data on the Florida pilot program were gathered from documents in the Navy Legal Assistance Office in Washington, D.C. and from interviews with Commander Robert Newton, at Pensacola, October 27, 1971, and Wilfred C. Varn, at Tallahassee, Florida, October 28, 1971.

in the case and "supervised" the work: The initial draft contained a more definitive eligibility rule—it was more stringent than OEO standards and consequently less threatening to the bar; even approval of noncourt work by out-of-state lawyers was sought. This was the only place this feature was sought. Beyond the accommodation of the Navy negotiator, the Florida Bar, for its part, immensely assuaged by strict eligibility standards, seemed to rise above parochial influences from both within that association and from the local bar associations in the area of the Naval Air Station, which felt most directly affected by the Navy program—the Escanbia-Santa Rosa County and the First Judicial Circuit Bar Associations. This, however, may have been an illusion. The Florida Bar negotiators recognized, from the outset, that Commander Newton was trying to work within the framework of the Integrated Bar Rule,[171] and that he thought people who were able to should pay.

Formal and first application was made directly to the state Bar.[172] There were extensive committee discussions, not just within the Military Liaison Committee, to which consideration of the pilot program was formally referred, but in other committees as well. There was more committee work in Florida than other states. Initial feelings and issues raised were not too different than those raised by the San Diego County Bar Association and others; the need for the program was questioned, as was the competence of military lawyers and the adequacy of their training to appear in Florida courts. The sincerity of the outer limits of eligibility was also questioned. There was a sense of accusation from the fact of the program itself, i.e., a sense that the bar was being accused of not discharging its past responsibilities to indigents, including servicemen. These feelings were aired and the Florida Bar ended its deliberations—which took nine months—by formally petitioning the Florida Supreme Court "For an Order to Allow a Member of a Bar, on Active Duty as a Judge Advocate of U.S. Navy, To Provide Legal Assistance to Certain Members of the Armed Services in the Pensacola, Florida Area." [173] It was felt that anything less than this action, in view of the integrated bar rule, would have produced an impasse.

---

[171] Report of Wilfred Varn, Chairman, Military Liaison Committee, Florida State Bar Association, January 29, 1971. *See* Article II.2 of the Integration Rule of the Florida Bar.

[172] Letter from Commander R.B. Newton to Burton Young, President, the Florida State Bar Association, January 4, 1971. A similar letter was sent to the Chief Justice of the Florida Supreme Court, but that was viewed by Commander Newton as advisory only. He was proceeding through channels. Interview with Commander Newton, October 27, 1971.

[173] In re: The Matter of Legal Assistance for Certain Members of the Armed

The Brief in Support of the Bar Petition said, in part:

The new Program is desirable and beneficial to all parties in interest as follows:

1. *The client* will deal with only one attorney with a common military background with resultant improved morale. There will be more rapid resolution of problems with a single attorney involved. Personal problems of eligible personnel will be resolved before these problems become disciplinary problems. Military personnel will be made aware that their parent service does have an interest in their well-being.

2. *The Military Services* will benefit by improved morale of its personnel, by reduction of potential disciplinary cases, and by less frustration on the part of military attorneys who may follow a case through to completion. Consequently, improved career retention rates should be realized on the part of personnel trained in military specialties, and the law, with more effective and efficient military forces resulting to the benefit of the United States.

3. *The Florida Bar* will benefit by removal of indigent charity cases concerning military personnel from its sphere of direct responsibility with a resultant increase in time available to devote to more productive cases and to local indigent cases. Clients who may not always be indigent but are presently eligible for assistance will be made aware of the legal services available in our complex society and will continue to appreciate the value of those services. Finally, the productive legal services within Florida will be increased.[174]

The brief appeared, in part, to be addressed to broad interests. However, when one considers the language in light of eligibility standards, it was not free from self-interest—indigency and eligibility explicitly appear to have been liberating factors. But, it cannot be said to rest entirely on self-interest. From discussions with members of the Florida Bar, it is apparent that the Bar—the Board of Governors, at least—was aware of implications of this petition that went beyond indigency and beyond the military program. The blanket approval of out-of-state lawyers for the military program, of course, sets precedent for OEO programs (New Jersey in reverse). What about out-of-state lawyers for approved group legal services (Florida has a group practice rule)? What about house counsel for Florida-based companies?

On October 13, 1971 the Florida Supreme Court entered the sought-for order, which provided in part:

Until June 30, 1973, a member of a Bar on active duty as a Judge Advocate of the United States Navy may act as attorney for and

---

Services, the Supreme Court of Florida, Case No. 41, 597, July Term, Order entered October 13, 1971.

[174] *Id.*

render legal assistance to certain enlisted personnel of the military services of the United States Armed Forces who might not otherwise be able to afford proper legal assistance subject to the *Rule Governing the Pilot Legal Assistance Program for Military Personnel* attached to and made a part of this Order.[175]

The "Eligibility" standards contained in the adopted Governing Rule provided:

B. The Basic Eligibility Standard for military personnel receiving legal assistance under this rule will be:

Is the applicant for legal service reasonably able to pay either set or contingent attorney's fees? If so, that applicant is not eligible for those services under this Legal Assistance Program.

C. Net Income Test:

1. Applicants whose net income shows a surplus in excess of Twenty-Five dollars ($25.00) per month, computed by deduction of all expenses from gross income, will be considered as providing an affirmative answer to the Basic Eligibility Standard . . . and *will not* be eligible for legal services under this Rule.

2. Applicants whose net income may be adjusted through counselling, reasonable budgeting methods, and purchase of basic needs only, to show a surplus in excess of Twenty-five Dollars . . . *will not* be eligible . . .

3. Married applicants in pay grades E–4 and below and single applicants in pay grades E–3 and below whose net income does not show and may not be adjusted to show a surplus in excess of Twenty-five Dollars ($25.00) per month . . . *will be* eligible . . .

[D. is a mechanism for appealing special cases to the Florida Bar]

E. Military personnel will not be eligible for legal services under the Rule if they possess the means to pay attorney's fees from personal sources outside of salaries paid by the Military Services . . .

F. A selected representative of The Society of the Bar of the First Judicial Circuit will have authority to pass on and veto the eligibility of applicants for the Program and no Navy lawyer may appear in court without first showing written evidence of approval of an applicant's eligibility by [such representative].[176]

The last provision is a close cousin to the local option in Kansas, but it applies on a case by case basis rather than to the program as a whole. (It is interesting that the term "veto" was used.) A look at the "eligibility standards" will tell the reader why the Navy in Washington and the other services are not happy with the Florida test. Moreover, with the recent pay raises, nobody is eligible for pilot program full services. Further, a look at the eligibility stand-

---

[175] *Id.*

[176] *Id.*, Rule Governing the Pilot Legal Assistance Program for Military Personnel, sec. IIB–IIF.

ards indicates what a high price was paid for the "approval" of "representation" by out-of-state lawyers—for the following:

> *IV Legal Assistance Officers*
>
> Clients receiving legal services pursuant to this Rule will receive full representation including, but not limited to, writing of letters, negotiations, preparation of documents and pleadings, and representation in litigation. Such full representation will be accomplished as follows:
>
> A. All representation, except appearances as attorney of record in Florida Courts, will be accomplished by [any lawyer designated by the Director of the law center as the "Florida Legal Assistance Officer.]
>
> B. Where appearance as attorney of record in Florida Courts is necessary, the applicant [sic] will be represented as follows:
>
> 1. If the Florida Legal Assistance Officer is a member of the Florida Bar, he will act as attorney of record.
>
> 2. If the Florida Legal Assistance Officer is not a member of the Florida Bar, *he will act as assistant counsel in association with a member of the Florida Bar,* who will appear as attorney of record. . . .[177]

When the court order is analyzed, the apparent bar cooperation seems to be an illusion. How seriously do the Rule's provisions about service models and eligibility standards reflect the statements made by the Florida Bar about the benefits of the program to the clients? The Florida rule (which in view of that state's integrated bar rule, its adoption of the Code of Professional Responsibility, and the extraterritorial status of the Naval Air Station may not have conferred anything) is a classic illustration of the double standards addressed in this study: Unauthorized practice of the law is perceived only in the precincts of professional economics. What is "full representation" to a poor client risks being called "inadequate representation" for those who can pay. What can be learned by the nonresident lawyer to assist the indigent serviceman,[178] or what can be supervised by Florida counsel, loses its efficacy if the client can pay. The order here is confusing, but so too is the unauthorized practice dilemma.

North Carolina: [179] The pilot program at Camp Lejeune does not exist. But, the local bar says that it does. This is not an illusion, as

---

[177] *Id.*, secs. IVA and IVB, 1 and 2.

[178] The training of legal assistance officers in Florida has been undertaken by reservists and the faculties of several Florida law schools.

[179] The data on North Carolina negotiations were gathered from reports in Washington, D.C., and interviews with Glenn L. Hooper, President of the Onslow County Bar Association, and Lt. Colonel Raymond W. Edwards, the Legal Assistance Officer at Camp Lejeune (Marine Corps Base). Both interviews were held on October 29, 1971 at Jacksonville, North Carolina.

in Florida. It is a delusion. What exists is a new legal aid society—the Onslow Legal Aid Association—where none existed before. The legal aid society takes special notice of military cases and military lawyers, allowing a little less cumbersome procedure for acceptance of military cases and a little "assistance" from the legal assistance officers.

The Onslow County Bar Association has 20 lawyer members. There are approximately 50 lawyers at the Marine Base. It is no surprise, therefore, that the local bar reacted negatively when confronted with the possibility of the pilot program. Military-community and military-bar relations had been strained before the suggestion of the pilot program. It did not help to have Marine negotiations conducted from Washington—from outside. Fear of economic loss was evident from the beginning as was the feeling that this was a "something for nothing program." Any thought of a pilot program handling criminal cases was quickly dispelled. In North'Carolina indigent criminal cases are handled by appointment, with the state paying the fees. In 1969–1970, 69 indigent criminal defense appointments were made in Onslow County, and the lawyers handling the appointments received $9,160 in fees. It was estimated that well over 90% of these cases involved military defendants.[180] Brigadier General Duane Faw, former Director of the Judge Advocate Division of the U.S. Marine Corps, agreed early in January 1971 to drop any request for criminal case coverage.

The Onslow County Bar Association met as a committee of the whole in February 1971 and considered three basic problem areas: (1) scope of service—i.e., type of cases, (2) definition of eligibility, and (3) the structure of the entity to handle the work. Committees were appointed for each area. The last problem area is central here—at no time did the Onslow County Bar Association consider that they would let the Marine Corps run its own program. The search was for an alternate way of handling the need, if any existed. The Onslow Legal Aid Association, a creature of the Onslow County Bar Association, was born. Its membership was restricted to County Bar members. It covered both civilian and military indigents. There appears to be some confusion as to whether it is a lawyer referral service or a legal aid society. In the "Policy" statements the by-laws state:

> No person other than a person who is without sufficient income or resources to employ private counsel shall be referred through the Association.[181]

---

[180] Interview with Glenn L. Hooper, October 29, 1971.

[181] Onslow Legal Aid Association, By-Laws, Article IV, sec. 2.

And Article V provides:

> In the event that it is decided that the person is without sufficient income or resources to employ private counsel, but is in a position to pay part of the fee, said person shall be required to make such payment on terms to be determined by the Association, to the attorney who handles the case.[182]

The mechanism for furnishing legal aid first requires that an applicant file an affidavit, which includes a statement of financial condition and an "agreement that if the applicant is assigned a legal aid attorney that the assigned attorney is not under any obligation to pursue the applicant's matter or case beyond the state that the same may be in at the time of such assignment."[183] The applicant must then contact *two* members of the Association requesting them each "to sign a statement that in his opinion the matter or case is a proper one for legal aid."[184] Then, the applicant shall deliver the affidavit and the two "certifications" "to the chairman of the Assignment Committee, and if the Assignment Committee shall agree that the matter or case is a proper one for legal aid it shall assign a member the same."[185] A high social cost and burden of entry is imposed on those seeking legal aid.

For the military indigent, the cost of entry is only slightly cheapened. A certification from the Marine Base legal assistance officer shall count for one sign-off—the military applicant still needs one more certification from a civilian lawyer before he can be assigned a civilian lawyer.[186]

Section 4 of the by-laws guards against the certification process being cheapened by paraprofessionals. It takes a lawyer—a member of the club—to operate the tests for eligibility. No one else can guard against diversion of bar income:

> No member of the Armed Services other than . . . an attorney . . . shall in any way directly or indirectly function, control or influence or attempt to do the same as to any or all of the certification procedural steps herein provided on any other matter or thing connected with the same.[187]

Article VII recognizes a role for the military lawyers:

> The assigned [civilian attorney] shall make use of the certifying military attorney to the extent that he shall determine in the handling of the matter or case.[188]

---

[182] *Id*, Article V.

[183] *Id.*, Article VI, Section 1.

[184] *Id.*, Article VI, Section 2.

[185] *Id.*, Article VI, Section 2.

[186] *Id.*, Article VI, Section 3.

[187] *Id.*, Article VI, Section 4.

[188] *Id.*, Article VII.

Presumably the "he" is the civilian lawyer. The delusion is complete—a pilot program which isn't, and a bar administered legal aid program which leaves considerable doubt about attachment to the model of service ahead of gain.

III. CONCLUSIONS

The military-bar negotiations in the several jurisdictions offered a unique opportunity for the organized bar to come to grips with the crucial questions implicit in the professional monopoly: Who is capable of representing a specific group of clients, for what kinds of matters, and under what circumstances? Unfortunately, as has been true too often, the opportunity was squandered. Preconceptions and pretense about competence and qualification frequently displaced meaningful concerns about "the clients." The holders of local licenses were treated to presumptions about their skills and capacities that were utterly absent from considerations of the skills and capacities of lawyers who held licenses in other jurisdictions. A double standard was involved. Issues of familiarity with local rules and practice, familiarity with the kinds of client problems encountered, availability of practical training and supervision, and amenability to discipline were hopelessly intertwined with concern about market protection and loss of income. The issue raised most persistently throughout the negotiations had to do with the economic level of the group to be served—about their ability to pay—and not the quality of the service that any client, rich or poor, would receive from any lawyer.

The local organized bars, for the most part, acted out the historical paradox: group legal services furnished by a group of young staff lawyers may be tolerable—albeit barely tolerable—to the organized bar for those clients who cannot afford to pay, but they are intolerable when distributed to the present paying clients of the organized bar. It is a paradox which has evident roots. But even where the organized bar is concerned about the well-being of the clients—here the military clients—that paradox hides a critical question: Has the organized bar's approach to the issues of training, competence, qualification, availability, supervision, and scrutiny of performance by professional peers assured any client, rich or poor, that he will be safeguarded against incompetence or misdirected services by locally admitted lawyers? Parochial concerns about license and about unauthorized practice of law have too often masked either the answers to that question, or, indeed, even the framing of the question. The present military-bar negotiations illustrate the process.

The strength of resistance to the pilot program was greater the closer the program came to a bar that considered that its livelihood was threatened. In some instances this resistance was assuaged by assurances of noncompetition; assurances which curiously also assuaged concern for the well-being of clients.

Principal representation by military lawyers often became more tolerable to the organized bar when it was coupled with arrangements for the appearance of locally admitted lawyers. That the role of the locally admitted counsel was in reality a secondary role—often analogous to that of Mr. Petrillo's stand-by musicians—was of little concern if words like "supervise," and "responsible" were used to describe the role. The assertion of the jurisdiction was important. More than face saving was involved. It was the maintenance of control over entry.

The organized bar exerts considerable control over the entire question of admissions—even temporary or special admissions. The courts, which have the inherent power to admit, have frequently surrendered much of that power to the bar. Presumably this partnership evolved so that the bar could exercise a stewardship over the profession, in the name of the public and in the name of the clients. It seems from our study that the bar's perception of this responsibility is by no means clear or central. Where client interest is involved there is confusion. In the case of indigent clients there may have even been abdication—witness the new legal aid societies which have been created in the wake of the threatened military legal assistance program. Frequently the confusion gave way to clarity—an unpleasant clarity: The client was not central at all; the profession was. Too often we saw a naked or barely disguised view that the law license is, or ought to be, a guarantee of income from a certified market area.

The military program is threatening. It is a socialized system for the delivery of legal services. The fractionalization of the group is unnatural. Accordingly, it does not cause actual dislocation of the present marketing arrangements for the distribution of legal services. There is no assurance that a group system is or can be the best way to deliver services, even to those who can pay. But, a review of that issue, from the viewpoint of the client, the society, and even the profession requires a thoughtful dialogue. The power of the legal profession to block that dialogue by veto is felt. If it is not real, at least the prestige element of the power—the presumed power—is enough to alter the dialogue. The military altered its plans for services to its group partly out of an analysis of bar power. Interests of clients must be balanced against interests of the profession, and if "profession" means anything, the interests of the client must be given greater weight. Lawyer dislocation is always possible—and probable.[189] There is a serious question, however, as to how a profession should react to that possibility: As a profession or as a trade union?

During the negotiations in the several pilot program jurisdictions the charge "creeping socialism" was frequently leveled at the military program as a way of ending thoughtful debate. The context of its use is descriptive of a view of lawyer role and license which I will typify by calling "creeping professionalism." This is a state of mind that disassociates the public utility aspects of the legal profession from the purpose and the function of the law license. It is a state of mind that paradoxically leaves the individual lawyer in a weaker position to independently render service to his client, free from outside influence, because he, too, looks to or is asked to look to a collective—the bar association—to protect him from the vicissitudes of the market. It is a state of mind that views the law license as analogous to a protective tariff. Neither pejorative usage is truly helpful. There is still the question of how best to meet the legal needs of the indigent military personnel and the nonindigent military personnel. For that matter, there remains the question: How are the legal needs of the public best met by the legal profession? Is the legal profession ready to face this question free from the pulls of parochialism, as a true profession—accepting the model of service ahead of gain?

---

[189] On the other side of the coin, client dislocation has not only been possible, it has been evident.